AWAY & HOME – WORLD WAR II

Somerset and Essex
1939 to 1945

by

PAT HERNIMAN

ACKNOWLEDGMENTS

First and foremost I want to thank Michael for his infinite patience and support and grandson Dean - a wizard with laptops! Also sister Jeanne Baker, Aunt Phyllis Bryant and cousins Geoffrey Prole and Don Wilson. The following also contributed: Andrew Berry (Sailing Barges Trust), Ronald Bond, Allen Buckroyd, Christine Day, Dennis Denyer, Linda Dyer (English Heritage), Wendy Eavis, Brian Evans, Doris Hill, Stephen Holland, John King, Glen Opie, T. Pennack Robin Reynolds, Alan Sheahan, Clive Smith and Mel Thompson. The following provided information and let me photograph items of interest. In particular, Local History Librarian Simon Donoghue of London Borough of Havering Local Studies Library for providing copies of maps and photos of war damage. Equally, Ian Hook at the Essex Regiment Museum for supplying material from the Leggett Collection and details of various aspects of the War and also Dot Bedenham who kindly provided escort for our visit to the Museum's store. Last, but not least, Margaret Stone/Brightlingsea Museum for her interest, help and encouragement and the staff at all the libraries who retrieved valuable information from the web.

Libraries: Great Baddow, Bightlingsea, Chelmsford Central and Maldon. Museums: 'Army Air Corps' Middle Wallop, 'Avoncroft' Kidderminster, 'Bakewell Old House', 'Battle of Britain' Capel le Ferne, 'Brightlingsea,' 'Combined Military Services' Maldon, 'Dulverton Heritage Centre', 'East Essex Aviation Society' Point Clear, 'Essex Regiment' Chelmsford, 'Flambards' Helston, 'Milestones' Basingstoke, English Heritage 'Tilbury Fort' & 'Great Yarmouth.' Schools: Havering Road Junior, now 'Parklands' (Viv Mangan Secretary and Pete Johnson IT Manager); Romford County High, now 'Frances Bardsley', (Rosemary Gaughan Deputy Head and Nelson Amoah Caretaker).

© Pat Herniman, 2016
Published by Papermill Books, Little Baddow,
in association with The Little Baddow History Centre
www.papermillbooks.co.uk

For Paul, Sandra, Craig, Dean,
& Christopher

* * *

and for young people world-wide,
we do so hope and pray for
'Peace in Their Time'

PREFACE

Pre-war trips to Romford library from an early age had turned me into a 'bookworm' but books generally during the war weren't easy to obtain. Damage to the library at RCHS 'Romford County High School for girls`, caused by a bomb dropped nearby in October 1941, had left them with very few. On a post war commercial course [1948/9] at South East Essex Technical College, I discovered the books of H.E. Bates, the first one being a slim volume entitled 'The Cruise of the Breadwinner', published 1946. Other books revealed the physical effects and mental emotional experiences gathered by him from RAF personnel during their recuperation breaks. Their pain and joy rekindled memories and I decided to record those of Michael and myself; many of which coincided. My ambition was to be put on a 'back burner` until his retirement in 1990 when we moved to Great Baddow. The prospect was daunting, but with help and encouragement from relatives, neighbours and friends I began collating and sorting material from various sources. The events are chronological and concurrent with military actions experienced by the Combined Forces and incidents which affected us on the 'Home Front.' The contents are an amalgam of information from many sources.

CONTENTS

* * *

I

ESCAPE TO THE COUNTRY

At the beginning of September 1939 Jeanne and I were evacuated privately from our home in Parkside Avenue, Romford in Essex to our maternal grandparents Harry and Annie Prole who lived at Kiln House in the village of Timberscombe in Somerset. We had made regular visits since we were tiny: in the very early days by motor bike and sidecar with Mum on pillion and Jeanne and I in the sidecar, later in a little Austin Seven saloon and by 1939 a 7 hp Jowett. I was looking forward to going into 'Junior' or as I thought of it the 'Big School' the next term and a visit to Gran and Grandad prior to this was an exciting prospect. We were always told the truth and Jeanne aged ten knew why we were going. As I was almost eight and a "why" child my parents had decided to spare me the forbidding news that German troops had occupied Poland.

Parkside Avenue

With no Service Stations we took our usual 'comfort stop' at Salisbury Plain near Stonehenge, which had been a regular camping area for our parents during their early trips. Dad made us all welcome cups of tea with our picnic primus stove. At the latter end of the journey I asked my usual question "When can we see the sea" and knew when we turned inland and up Dunster Steep we would soon reach Timberscombe. Gran and Grandad welcomed their 'little maids' and we were happy to see them, but this time I was anxious when Mum and Dad eventually set off for home without us. Three weeks in Gt. Ormond Street hospital at the age of three, with no visits or communication allowed, had made me vulnerable to separation, but at Kiln House we were lucky to be with family. It was more challenging for official evacuees, three million of whom were being sent to complete strangers in various parts of Britain in Operation "Pied Piper". It was recorded that by 2nd September 485,900 had already reached their destinations; their luggage being restricted to a spare set of underwear in a small case, their gas masks and a favourite toy. Beccles in Suffolk was our 'allotted' destination where we would have made different friends.

Jowett

After breakfast on the sunny morning of Sunday 3rd, Uncle Bob took us for a walk down to Cowbridge where he lived with the Yeandle family in the lodge at the entrance to Knowle Park owned by Lady Constance Ryder and her sister. The cricket ground there was a popular venue for the Prole family who were all great enthusiasts: Uncles Bob and Harry were bowlers and Cecil an umpire. The team was soon to be depleted and older men and young lads were to replace those called up. On that historical morning we all sat down in front of the wireless and at 11.15 am a serious voice made a solemn announcement that we were at war with

8

Germany. The grown-ups had known for sometime that it was inevitable, but I was too young to understand the full implications and was anxious when Mrs. Yeandle cried as I realised it must be bad news.

Stonehenge

Kiln House

Evacuees from Tottenham who had travelled by train were to arrive later that day and were billeted with local families. It was to alter the lives of so many people for the next six years and families would have to learn to adapt to many changing circumstances. Gran, like so many mums of her age, had already experienced Grandad and two elder sons serving in WWI and coping with the remaining younger children. Uncle Bob didn't make the grade for call-up in WWII and carried on his job as a gardener, but Uncle Cecil was to volunteer and Uncle Harry to be enlisted.

Knowle Lodge

We didn't have much time to dwell on things in such a busy household: we soon settled in and I celebrated my 8th birthday on the 9th. Late season holidaymakers taking advantage of the lovely weather asked Jeanne and I about cream teas and we directed them to Kiln House where the parlour by the side entrance was kept ready and Gran always had freshly baked scones, clotted cream and home-made jam available. One of the first activities Jeanne and I witnessed was the harvesting in a nearby field and I felt sorry for the bunnies who dashed out with bobbing tails, weaving their way to the hedges as their cover vanished in diminishing circles. The sheaves of corn in bundles of six were lined up across the field resembling miniature golden wigwams. When sufficiently dried they were collected for threshing and the subsequent straw bales forked rhythmically onto wagons and taken off to be built into a stack. Times have changed and now giant plastic clad 'pillbox' shaped bales await removal by forklifts. The diminishing stack was beaten at regular intervals to eliminate rats foraging for seed and, although I didn't like them, I had mixed feelings because I knew they must have had homes and families nearby who would miss them. I was missing mine who were some two hundred miles away. By 1940 the rat countrywide population was reckoned at around five million and 2d. a tail was offered for each one eliminated. Volunteers countrywide and the W.L.A "Women's Land Army" took on the task, no doubt happy to increment their low wages.

Harvesting

The 29th of September was Registration day when 65,000 enumerators had the enormous task of carrying out the necessary enquiries for the whole country: Jeanne's number being 'WQCE/107/7' and mine ending in '8' [The 'WQ' I assume denoting 'West Quantocks'?] Gran also accepted a boy named Alvis Bentley Carter from Grays in Essex as he and his parents had been regular Bed & Breakfast visitors. Gran and Grandad were then aged sixty-four and it was quite a commitment for them to take on three of us. Alvis was so embarrassed when I asked him his name that I tried hard not to mention it, as I felt so sorry for him. I assume his father wanted the initials 'ABC' to head the list of second hand car dealers in the classified section of telephone directories.

Built of local warm pink sandstone, 'Kiln' was a combination of two houses with access inner doors connecting both. With three bedrooms in

11

each it was just about large enough to accommodate the extended family. The door fronting the main street has since been blocked up. This led straight into the dining/living room, which was the hub of the household where we all congregated. There were no fridges in those days but the larders at the back were cool even in warmer weather. The shelves were crowded, with jugs of milk with crocheted covers with beaded edges, butter in a large terracotta dish with water in its base and a muslin covered cheese board. Other shelves held jars of whortleberry or marrow and ginger jam, bottled fruit, pickled onions and cabbage. Domed wire meshed covers protected leftover meat and a flat iron weighted down plated brawn. On the floor stood a sack of flour and another of cornmeal with a scoop for feeding the free-range chickens in the yard who always supplied us with plenty of fresh eggs. Grandad reared two pigs a year so they always had plenty of bacon etc. One joint hung from a hook in the ceiling whilst another was curing in packed salt in a wooden tub with brass handles.

As they had no electricity at Kiln, Uncle Ray Bryant, husband-to-be of Aunt Phyl, rigged up wiring with two accumulators to give enough power for two lamps downstairs and the wireless. These were charged weekly at Loveridge's sweet shop up the hill past the church. Candles and oil lamps provided the rest of our lighting; the latter needing regular topping up, mantles replaced, wicks trimmed and the brass polished. Gran declined my eager offer to help with whortleberry picking on nearby Croydon Hill, "up over" as she called it, anticipating more would be crushed than collected! Her pies were delicious with clotted cream. She was a very good cook and our meals included roast chicken, marrows stuffed with mince and various rabbit dishes. Grandad set snares for them and Uncle Cecil had two ferrets. The day I accompanied him a baby bunny dashed out of a hole and I asked to have it as a pet. He managed to catch it but after a short distance told me it would miss its mummy. As I was missing mine I agreed it should be freed and hoped it would find its way back home. It was difficult, however, not to think about it as portions appeared regularly on my plate. I had mixed feelings too about the ferrets, but when the weather got colder I offered to knit woollies for them. Assured by Gran they wouldn't need them I lavished my affection on her dog "Rival" and we soon became good friends.

During the week breakfast was taken in relays to fit in with work and school times, but at weekends it was more relaxed. I have always liked observing people and I remember on one occasion watching Uncle Harry sitting alone to eat his breakfast, gazing into long distance seemingly oblivious of what was going on around him. I wondered what he was thinking about but didn't like to interrupt his reverie. Being a large household it was difficult for individuals to find somewhere for quiet contemplation and he had obviously acquired the knack of shutting himself off. When the whole family lunched together on Sunday we had just enough room around the large solid oak dining table. The removable top was plain one side for working purposes and polished on the reverse and it took two uncles to turn it at the end of the day. [Historically, the turning had been to indicate 'unwanted visitors not welcome'.] Being a chatty child I'd been taught not to interrupt and found this difficult at Sunday lunchtime with all the family present. Whilst awaiting an opportunity to 'dive in' I watched the flies orbiting lazily around the light fitting but didn't enjoy witnessing their struggles when they stuck to the dangling flypaper like blackcurrants. Eventually, having asked permission to leave the table, I slid from my chair to go elsewhere to amuse myself. Gran who had already brought up five girls and five boys was always firm but fair about behaviour and we'd been well schooled at home.

Most of the evacuees from Tottenham soon settled. I didn't know at the time that that they had been selected which probably explains a very quiet and polite boy named David being allocated to the Old Mill [eventually he was to become an antique dealer.] Aunt Kath's mother-in-law Mrs. Ray had a preference for boys: not girls who found it difficult 'to be seen and not heard'! I expect the farmers preferred muscular boys, particularly at harvest time. The villagers shared their experiences with Aunt Kath and she was told by friends that some of their charges cried every night and others wet their beds. Because of their restricted luggage they soon needed extra clothing especially when the particularly cold winter arrived. We were so fortunate to be with our relatives and not having to make such an adjustment and got on well with the newcomers as they were good natured, had a sense of humour and we soon got used to being teased. I decided not to repeat a dubious rhyme recited by one of the boys as I didn't understand it. Because Jeanne and I weren't official evacuees, the authorities decided we should attend school with the village children. We soon became firm friends and, having learned a lot from them about country life, Jeanne and I soon became 'Country Mice'. The old schoolhouse built in the 1800's still survives. I got to school early and enjoyed ringing the turreted bell.

We had lessons in the morning and Nature Rambles or Country Dancing in the Reading Room in the afternoon; the evacuees with their two teachers vice versa. Some seventy years later, Michael and I were to meet Ena one of the Tottenham evacuees who also lives in Great Baddow. At Timberscombe we had only two classes with the Infants being taught by Miss Mary Land and the Juniors by Mrs. Willis the Headmistress. Jeanne and I were in the latter and it must have been a challenge for our teachers to encompass the varying ages. Dad had taken us regularly to Romford Library for books for extra reading enjoyment and we had both been taught basic arithmetic by Mum before starting school. At Timberscombe I struggled with long division £.s.d. as I had only just been introduced to it back home in the last year of Infant school: if only they'd had metric in those days! In sewing lessons we made gingham aprons, but I didn't need tuition for knitting as Mum had already taught me before I started school.

Timberscombe school

I really enjoyed the Nature Rambles as we were surrounded by beautiful countryside, which included a good view of Dunkery Beacon on Exmoor. One day we were told to throw ourselves under the hedgerow to practise evasion from possible attacks by low flying aircraft. After a brief protest from Jeanne and I about the mass of stinging nettles, we flung ourselves dutifully under the hedge with the others and then rushed to pick dock leaves to put on our smarting legs. As the lovely late summer came to an end we entered the Season of 'mists and mellow fruitfulness' so beautifully described in Keat's poem 'Autumn'. The hills of Exmoor changed hue as the bracken turned to brown and the heather faded. The leaves on trees and hedgerows changed to beautiful shades of yellow, gold, bronze and red and looked lovely in the afternoon sunshine. At sunset, the fading light as the sun slid down behind Dunkery Beacon on Exmoor, slowly transformed the sandstone walls of Kiln House to a deeper, glowing pink. The song "Sunset down in Somerset, brings back dreams I can't forget ..." describes it all. I loved sketching and painting the twigs and leaves brought back to school from the Nature Rambles; particularly the contrasting colours of the brown stalks and waxen pink berries of the spindlewood tree. We also picked ripened hazel nuts along the wayside and cracked them between our teeth. I'm sure a dentist wouldn't have approved!

Autumn tints

After school Jeanne and I were allowed to wander at will. We kept quiet in order to observe the wild life as the slightest sound would send a stoat or weasel scurrying for cover. On one occasion we spied a bright-eyed field mouse in a bank nearby having a snack and were amazed by the volume of sound produced by a tiny wren with upturned tail. Sometimes we went with Grandad to his designated allotment at Kiln Orchard, which was at Bickham along the Dulverton road. I skipped alongside trying to keep up with his long strides and asked lots of questions. I remember still the many signs and sayings of impending weather conditions which he taught us. The allotment on a raised bank above the lane also had a cider apple tree. He pointed out the entrance to a badger's home and I imagined it with its family somewhere beneath our feet. Whilst he collected vegetables, Jeanne and I collected the cider apple windfalls and soon discovered how sharp they were. I didn't know then that badgers like apples otherwise I would have left some for them. We returned to Kiln House laden with the fresh greens and potatoes; ready for the pot and so

15

tasty. The pig enjoyed his share of the apples and the uncles the cider from Grandad's press, which was housed in the cowshed across the yard. Aunt Phyl has since told us told us that Grandad padlocked the press to prevent 'surreptitious sips', but Uncle Cecil had drilled a hole through the cork to suck some up through a straw! One day I wandered into the cowshed, the tap was free and I couldn't resist the temptation to sample some. I knew I should have asked first and blushed even more when my flushed cheeks prompted Gran to asked me if I was all right!

Michael also has roots in Somerset and we have made regular visits. One autumn we located the allotment, which I recognised immediately. It was no longer cultivated but one ancient cider apple tree still remained. Not pruned for many years it had gnarled and stooping shoulders but had managed to produce some apples, which were hanging from its upper branches which was amazing after over seventy years. It's sad to think they may not have been harvested after all its effort, but maybe some badgers were to enjoy them? Memories came flooding back and brought a lump to my throat as my thoughts travelled back to 1939 when the tree was in its prime and we had been able to reach the lower branches to pick the apples.

Jeanne and I also enjoyed walking down to Cowbridge off the main road past Huxtable's petrol pumps. Here we played 'Pooh Sticks', dropping twigs into the river Avill and dashing to the other side to see which came out first and counting our victories. We found too, if we hung over the parapet of the bridge, the flow of the water beneath made us feel we were moving forward: similar to sitting in a stationary carriage with an adjacent train moving off in the opposite direction. It was a calming experience watching shoals of fish keeping station under the bridge and then with quick flicks of their tails darting off to another spot. Beethoven's 6th, Pastoral symphony, 'scene when arriving in the country' and 'scene by the brook' are evocative.

One Saturday morning when Jeanne was still helping Gran I set off with a village toddler whose mother had given permission for her to join me. On our return from Bickham I declined the offer of a lift from a male motorist because Jeanne and I, when very young, had been advised not to. Other times after school we accompanied Olive Stevens who lived at West Harwood farm up off the Cutcombe and Dulverton road. We all called loud "hellos" across the Avill valley to hear our voices return and Jeanne and I soon mastered the call which brought the cows down to the five barred gate to be driven up to the farm for milking. At close quarters they were enormous and I watched anxiously as they lurched heavily in and out of the hole made by the propping post of the gate.

Cowfield below West Harwood

View from Totterdown

On other days we went home with Brenda Quartly who lived at 'Totterdown' farm on the main Minehead road from which there are lovely views to the hills across the valley. We watched the various stages of processing after milking and I remember the clacking of the butter churn and the trays of thick, crusted clotted cream cooling in the dairy.

17

We were allowed to feed some of the young weaning calves from a bucket of warm milk and, with our hands cupped just under the surface with fingers extended upwards, we watched as they licked the milk off with their rough little tongues. They were so pretty close range with wide nostrils, big brown eyes, long lashes and I could feel the soft little bumps protruding from their foreheads when I stroked them. Not far from Kiln House, Miss Eva Floyd made home-made ice cream. The container, in a bucket of water surrounded by ice, was placed outside a nearby neighbour's cottage where it could be seen from the road. [This wouldn't pass today's 'Health & Safety' standards!] We watched fascinated as she dispensed ice cream between wafers, or with equal expertise placed dollops into cornets. I preferred the latter and would nibble around the cornet pushing the ice cream down with my tongue until I had a miniature cornet at the finish.

Milk churn

18

Miss Floyd's row

At school we had mid morning biscuits and milk and, as autumn receded and winter approached, it was heated slowly in a large saucepan on the stove during lesson time acquiring a thick skin in the process. When it was poured out my tummy heaved as I saw great lumps of skin plopping out into the mugs. Not wanting to appear a 'wimp' I'd swirl it round with my finger or pencil and, with my eyes shut, take a deep breath and try to gulp it down without stopping! At lunchtime, Jeanne and I only had to cross the road for the short walk back to Kiln House. I can still visualise Gran standing at the range stabbing sausages and putting them into the large frying pan. She was short and homely and shaped like a 'cottage loaf'. Wearing a wrap-around sleeveless drawstring overall and with her grey hair drawn up in a bun with stray wisps at the neck, she reminded me very much of Mrs. Tiggy Winkle from one of Beatrix Potter's books which were my favourites. Claude Bishop used to join us with his sandwiches, as he didn't have time to get home to Oaktrow Farm some distance from the village off the Dulverton road. They had been neighbours when Gran and Grandad were at Slade Farm before moving down to Timberscombe.

Aunt Phyl helped a lot at Kiln House when not at the local shop. Once a week she washed the flagstone floor of the main room, starting at the front door and throwing buckets of water which she swept with a broom to the step down into the scullery at the back. Jeanne black-leaded the range on Saturday mornings and I blancoed the front doorstep, which was invisible at night as they had no street lighting. Gran had probably decided that if I spilled any Blanco it would be easier to clean me and the road! Indoors I dusted the things I could reach which didn't include the ornaments on the mantelpiece high up over the range. The two china hearth dogs, put there out of harm's way, had been given to Gran and Grandad by two uncles who had picked mushrooms to pay for them. We now have the pleasure of owning them and they bring back fond memories. Grandad spent quite a lot of his spare time at a block in the yard chopping large logs from a stack whilst Jeanne and I stood well back, watching with bated breath and peeping through our fingers until he reached the last piece held by his fingertips. When the final two pieces splintered away from the block we ran to collect them all. The smell of wood smoke always reminds me of Somerset. There was a constant demand for kindling and chunks for both the range and the wood-burning wash boiler in one of the outhouses. Dual purpose, this had a capacity for ten Christmas puddings and was also used for ham joints. Gran`s little hands were puffy from constant immersion with the loads of washing and, because the scullery tap only had cold water, a kettle was always simmering on top of the range in the main room for hot water, with the oven below ready for cooking joints and baking scones and cakes etc. Flat irons with rags wrapped around the handles were heated on the top, with others on brass stands on the floor being moved up to the range when needed for the regular mounds of ironing. I was always rushing around and one day tripped over a flagstone and hurtled towards the range. Putting both hands out to avoid landing bodily on it, I then ran instinctively to the cold-water tap to cool down my scorched palms.

The Rev. Isidore Lach-Szyrma visited for occasional evening chats with Gran: maybe he was a Polish refugee with an empathy for evacuees? The loaded clothes horse was often in front of the range and, on bath nights, provided a screen when the aluminium tub was brought in and put in front of it. One evening when he called in I crouched quietly until he left. Aunt Phyl has told us that she had her bath in the dairy, which was freezing cold in the winter. At the end of the week Gran sat by the door for the uncles to put their pay packets on to her lap for deduction of their keep. In their leisure time they were skilful at the Red Lion's skittle alley. Gran and Grandad didn't relax until the evenings when they'd top up the range with coal from the scuttle and settle in their chairs at either end to rest or read the paper. Jeanne and I sat up at the table to read or draw until it was bedtime. Bronzed from working outside Grandad always wore a cap and kerchief to keep the sun off his head and neck and I can remember his white bald head shining in the lamplight as he bent forward and I stood on my toes to reach his forehead to kiss him goodnight. I went up to bed at 7 pm and, as daylight shortened, needed a candle to light my way through the latched door to climb the "timber hills" as they were called and walk the length of the wide landing to reach our bedroom.

Granny Baker's kitchen (Courtesy of Dulverton Heritage Centre)

Whilst I waited for Jeanne who came up at 7.30 pm I watched the candlelight's flickering shadows on the walls and hoped she wouldn't be long and we could snuggle up together in the cosy bed. With no central heating it was a comforting way to sleep and I felt safe with her. For our personal washing facilities we had a marble-topped washstand with a matching set of china bowl, jug and soap dish. The chamber pot or gazunder [we called it a "goes under" as it was kept under the bed] was emptied the next morning into a lidded slop bucket. It was particularly useful during the cold winter as it was a long way to the privy at the end of the yard! Occasionally Uncle Harry's future wife Bessie Cadwallader slept with us. She had a soft, gentle Welsh voice and I remember her in the candlelight loosening and brushing her long hair, kneeling silently to say her prayers, blowing out her candle and then easing gently into bed trying not to disturb us. Jeanne and I said our prayers under the warm covers: I had a simple one that Mum had taught us and I always finished with "Please let Mummy and Daddy live a long time". When women filled vacancies left by servicemen, Aunt Bessie was to drive a delivery van for the main bakery in Minehead. Sunday didn't have such a strict timetable and, before winter set in, it had been nice to lie in bed watching the curtains drifting out of the open window and listen to the bells of St. Petrock across the way ringing out for Matins. It is a lovely church, mostly l5th century, the first vicar being listed as Ralph de Soutre in l313. St. Petrock is the patron saint of the stag and they still abound in the neighbouring hills. The bells were to become silent in 1940 and only to be used as the warning of an Invasion. [The ban was to be lifted on 4th November 1942 to celebrate the victory at El Alamein: considered to be the turning point of the War.]

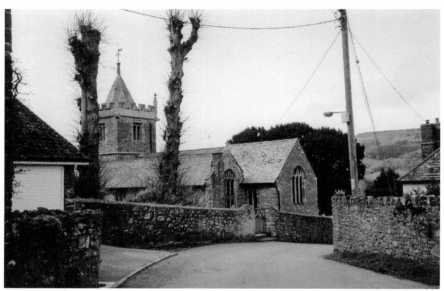

St. Petrock's

The milking shed at Kiln was just across the yard and we were allowed to climb the ladder into the loft to play amongst the sweet smelling hay. This was great fun and the day we lingered I remember Gran calling anxiously from the scullery door. It seems like yesterday: since then the sheds have been converted into holiday lets. The cows came to be milked at regular intervals; their heavy bulk swaying as they picked their way across the cobbles. One day, with permission, I squatted on a stool and with my head resting on the cow's side managed to produce a little but my fingers were too small. I was thankful, however, that the 'gentle giant' towering above me didn't seem to mind. Evacuees from London liked to watch and one day a boy was offered a drink. With one knee bent and head to one side he had some of the warm liquid squirted directly into his mouth. I don't think he enjoyed it as he pulled a face and shook his head as it went down. I liked the cows as they were very sociable and I remember an occasion when one, having been milked, wandered down to peer at me through the small curtained window of the privy in the yard.

Cowshed

Being a small village we got to know the locals fairly quickly. Maurice Stoodley's house was next to us, and then Mr. Jefferys the grocer.

Jefferys shop

As we stepped down into his shop we could smell all the items he stocked as they weren't double-wrapped in those days: tea, coffee, soap etc. and also paraffin, candles, bundles of kindling. I particularly remember the glass topped square tins of biscuits along the front edge of the counter and the mixed broken ones at the right hand end, which were cheaper.

Aunt Phyl worked at the shop next door to Burnell's the butcher; just across from the 'Lion' public house. The shop stocked almost everything and, as she did most of the preparation work, she had to be there by 7 am. She jointed half a pig and boiled it ready for the slicer and stripped the muslin off the half cwt. of cheese ready for the board with wire cutter. At the rear of the shop were bulk supplies of sugar, coffee and tea, which she weighed up into bags and there were also sacks of cornmeal. Bolts of checked cotton material were also available: these were slapped open across the counter, the required yardage counted and cut across from the folded edge. As most cottages had deep window recesses, any remnants were fashioned with pinking shears into edging for their ledges and also tray cloths and jam pot covers.

Ex shop in Timberscombe

Jeanne and I went up the hill via the 'Lion' inn to Mrs. Loveridge for sweets. Shaken from glass-topped jars they clattered noisily into the pan of the scales and were tipped into a cone-shaped paper bag and spun round: the ears and tapered base reminiscent of the TV 'Wombles'. We also looked forward to our regular pocket money and Callard & Bowser Cream Line toffees and chewy mints from Mum and Dad as they made us feel 'at home'. The other four shops catered for most needs, but now the village has a by-pass, Minehead Supermarkets have taken over and the shops have reverted to living accommodation. Mr. Cole the saddler had his premises at the rear of Kiln House with access via a small bridge over the river Avill from the main road to Dunster.

Before the winter set in Mum and Dad paid a visit bringing our Christmas presents and warmer clothing which included liberty bodices with suspenders, fashioned knitted stockings, a dress for Jeanne and two-piece for me. Mum must have spent every spare minute to achieve that. Knitting is therapeutic and when Dad was on night shift it must have been helpful and I am sure her love was looped into every stitch. At Kiln our presents were tucked away and we discovered years later that they had also brought our party dresses to wear at Christmas, but the winter of '39/'40 was to be much too cold. Jeanne and I were overjoyed to see our parents. I'd had a recent tumble and, whilst they were with us, Uncle Ray changed a dressing on my festering knee. As he whipped off the sticking lint I let out a word I'd picked up from the evacuees and immediately clapped my hand over my mouth. My mother was shocked but Uncle Ray managed to keep a 'straight face'! We went to school on the morning they left and at break time asked for permission to see them before they set off. Mrs Willis agreed reluctantly and we ran to Kiln House where we clung to them pleading to be taken home too. When they left Uncle Ray carried me on his shoulders around the house in an effort to console me. Jeanne too was very comforting and this helped a lot. They had brought the mother of Alvis with them and when she came on a subsequent visit we were to be chastised and told that Mum had cried all the way back to Essex and we were sad.

Shortly before Christmas I had been to Poole's shop and with my pocket money bought a blue glass cruet set for Mum and a packet of ten Gold Flake cigarettes for Dad. I packed them very carefully and took the parcel to the Post Office. Mum told me later that Dad had kept the cigarettes for some time. It was our first Christmas away from home and all the family crowded around the table for the traditional roast chicken, Christmas pudding and mince pies. We enjoyed ourselves as all the aunts and uncles made it as happy as they could for us, but we missed our parents so much.. At home we had always listened to King George VI's Christmas broadcast but we didn't hear it at Kiln as they probably thought it would upset us. It wasn't an easy speech for him to make and must have taken courage. He quoted from Louise Haskins 'The Desert': "Give me a light that I may tread safely into the unknown ... put your hand into the hand of God ... better than light and safer than a known way." The war years must have been a tremendous burden for him and people of our generation are grateful for his dedication to duty.

We regularly visited Aunt Kath at the Old Mill; either by the river Avill along Gt. House Street: called 'Duck Street' as so many of them waddled up from the river, or uphill past Loveridge's and the church, after which we scampered down the stone steps at the side of the Methodist Chapel. The Mill had a mounting block to one side of the entrance and an old grinding stone propped upright on the other. Having called "coo-ee" through the top half of the door, which was always open, we awaited her reply and then stepped down into the cool and dim interior. It was a massive room with a flagstone floor where originally flour had been stored. It housed the machinery, which turned the giant water wheel outside and I remember watching the water cascading off when Mr. Ray set it working to keep it in order. The cool atmosphere was ideal for the trays of eggs from Aunt Kath's chickens, which she kept in the orchard up the lane. A house has since been built on that site which has a beautiful view to Dunkery Beacon on Exmoor. With our dresses scooped up we had paddled in the river during the warmer weather, but in the winter we enjoyed the welcoming cups of cocoa and biscuits, which Aunt Kath provided. She reminded us years later how we liked to spoon out the first mixture of cocoa powder, sugar and milk whilst the kettle heated up. Their lodger Mr. Geeson and old Mr. Ray sat at the table by the range. Mr. Geeson had a squeaky voice caused by gas attacks during WWI and we had to shout when talking to the latter as he had been deafened by howitzers. He had bushy whiskers and looked like 'Old Bill' the WWI poster character. He sat with an elbow on the table cupping his ear in his hand to catch what we were saying. He still had his trunk from the war in one of the eight bedrooms. The mill is a large rambling building and is said to date back to the early 1800s, but Uncle Ern told us that the old barn was much earlier. The property has changed a lot and now has en suite bedrooms. Old buildings have atmosphere and it's nice to visit them and recall the past, but the Old Mill has changed so much that I prefer to remember it as it was.

Aunt Kath was always busy with so much to cope with, but her brassware was always gleaming, the lamps regularly cleaned and the place spick and span. They too had no electricity and the main room beyond the working area only had a small window, which meant oil lamps were lit quite early. The loo upstairs had no light, which meant leaving the door open, but that and the downstairs one had flushes; no doubt fed direct from the river. Their garden produced a wonderful display of sweet peas and runner beans. They had a spinet in the kitchen/living room on which Uncle Ern's mother taught me to play "We`ll meet again", but my thumb and little finger couldn't span the longer gaps. She wouldn't listen to the news bulletins and I realise now that she was trying to shut off from reality and the song must have given her some comfort.

Old *Mill*

Uncle Ern was enrolled into the RAMC, "Royal Army Medical Corps", and was to be involved in many traumatic situations. The hospital ship the 'Duke of Rothesay' was to be in constant escort attendance during many engagements including the North Atlantic Convoys with vital supplies for Russia when ships suffered appalling weather conditions, which shifted tanks on their decks causing many injuries amongst crew members.

The 'Rothesay' was also to bring back the first casualties of the 'D-Day' Landings and finally the casualties to a medical station in India. He told us later of the wonderful scenery from the foothills of India. He was finally to return to England during the summer of 1946. He and Aunt Kath had been married in the summer of 1940. She recalled a scary experience in the 'Battle of Britain' when a crippled German bomber flew low over the mill and along the Avill valley in an endeavour to find a landing area; probably having been damaged by the guns sited on the Brendon hills. She watched from her bedroom window as the plane crash-landed. Three baled out crew members walked down into the village to surrender; the remaining two, presumably the pilot and navigator, were found by

27

villagers who discovered one of them literally hung by his neck in the fork of a tree. Could the pilot have teen trying to avoid to avoid crashing on the village? I am sure their pilots had mixed feelings about their duties. Our friend Chris Day told us recently that her mother recalled waving to a pilot flying low along the river Crouch at Burnham in Essex. After he had waved back she realised the plane was German.

Although West Somerset was not a strategic target itself, German planes were to fly over it from occupied France, probably Cherbourg, to bomb targets in the Cardiff and Bristol areas. Aunt Phyl too was to have a nasty experience at Watchet. Hearing gunfire whilst hanging out her washing she assumed it was the usual gunnery practice at nearby Donniford Camp, but glancing up she saw the pilot's face and the swastikas on the low-flying plane and dashed for her kitchen door. The plane went on to crash at Porlock Weir.

To return to Timberscombe ... The winter of 1939/40 was really cold; recorded as the coldest winter for forty years. We appreciated the warm clothing our parents had brought us. Distant Exmoor's heather and bracken became covered with a mantle of snow and, when the roads turned to ice underfoot, Gran tied rags around Jeanne's shoes to go to school. I was to be housebound for several days with a cold and looked out to see the snow gradually disappearing knowing that I was missing out on sliding down the snow clad field at Bickham Manor on toboggans provided by Mr. Morell for the enjoyment of the children in the village.

Bickham Manor

At Christmas the publishers Hodder and Stoughton, presented each London evacuee with one of their books. We soon resumed our walks back to West Harwood Farm after school and eventually saw the first snowdrops with beautiful markings poking out from the remaining pockets of snow. "Snowdrop Valley" is now a popular tourist attraction.

Snowdrops

Having lived in a town we had really enjoyed the scenery and different moods of the countryside so well captured in the hymn "All things bright and beautiful" which may well have been written from a viewpoint on Grabbist hill above Dunster. W.H. Davies' poem "Leisure", "What is life if, full of care, we have no time to stand and stare…" also describes the beauty of the countryside. They depict all the things we could enjoy whilst away and I feel guilty now that I didn't appreciate enough the wonderful sights, sounds and sensations we experienced, but at the time our minds were so often distracted by thoughts of home. In Essex we lived in suburbia with neat housing, tarred roads and public parks and, in peacetime, could soon drive out to the countryside, but Somerset was even better as it was all around us and we had been able to rub shoulders with Nature and observe its wonderful changes as the seasons progressed.

The so called "Phoney War" tempted some evacuees to return home, but some who preferred the country life would eventually decide to remain for good which must have caused tremendous heartaches for all those concerned. We were grateful for the loving care of our grandparents, but Jeanne told our parents that if we had to die she wanted us to be together as a family and, with misgivings, we were fetched home to become "Town Mice" once more. For years I wondered if I would ever meet any of the London evacuees until, seventy years later, whilst waiting for a bus into Chelmsford, we chatted with someone who told us she had been evacuated to Timberscombe. She also used our road en route to the local surgery at Great Baddow and had the same doctor.

II

FROM BLISS TO BLITZ

Preparations for Hostilities

Once back home to Parkside Avenue Romford we soon settled into our usual routine and Jeanne remembers we had our hair bobbed short again. I was unaware that I had acquired a distinct west county accent whilst away until the boy next door asked me "why are you talking funny?" The official evacuees from our area had been sent to Beccles in Suffolk so I would have acquired a distinctly different accent. The children from London, billeted in the East Anglian coastal area were to be moved elsewhere when Hitler started making plans for invasion when France capitulated and heavy bombing ensued in that region.

On our return from Somerset, Jeanne and I had resumed lessons at Havering Road School, now named "Parklands", where she finished her final year and I entered the second year Juniors. Entries in the school log record the following events covering the days immediately prior to and the time during which we were in Somerset.

"Aug. 29th 1939 - Air raid shelters are being constructed in Playing Field."

"Sept. 3rd - Owing to the outbreak of hostilities the school has been closed today for a week in accordance with Government Broadcast instructions."

"Sept. 11th - School to remain closed until further instructions are received."

"October 25th - From today and until such time as the Air Raid shelters in the playground are completed, the children in the 3rd and 4th years will attend in half classes each half hour for the purpose of receiving school work to be done in their homes, and for handing in completed work for correction by the teachers."

"Nov. 1st - An emergency scheme of education for the children in the lst and 2nd Years has been commenced today. The children, whose parents wish them to participate in the scheme, have been divided into 45 groups which will meet in various private houses where rooms are available."

95 Parkside Avenue

We had been unaware of all this in Somerset. The mixed age class there had been a disadvantage to Jeanne who had to take her scholarship exam whilst evacuated: the curriculum in some aspects was different and in the geography section the questions were on the West Country. Some time ago an education programme highlighted the difficulties of her age group during the War. In her particular case the relevant authorities in Somerset had obviously not been informed that we were from Essex and had been in a class with 'locals'. Being in a mixed age class was also a distinct disadvantage: I had been struggling and she was being held back. Illnesses in her early years had also deprived her of a lot of schooling whereas I had them before starting and had only missed the few weeks' quarantine when she had diphtheria three years before the outbreak of hostilities. She had lots of catching up to do and missed a place at High School, but the proximity of Pettits Lane school, now "Marshalls Park", was to be a great advantage when aerial bombardment began.

Moving on to wider aspects of the War: having been appointed First Lord of the Admiralty in 1939, Winston Churchill then became Chief of Staff including the Service Ministers in early April 1940. At Buckingham Palace on 10th May King George VI requested him to form a Coalition Government and Churchill then began the tremendous task of leading us through the next five years of hazardous wartime conditions and was an inspiration to us all. Older people had been invited to help with the war effort and eventually 70,000 pensioners were to be involved. Those with building skills were sought after and Michael's maternal grandfather George Lambert, an experienced Master Carpenter, volunteered his services. A youthful seventy-five, he reversed his age and was soon scaling lofty ladders into the roof space of aircraft hangars. He was used to this as he had been employed in the construction of Exhibition Halls in Europe and also the one at Wembley in 1924. A man of great determination he didn't give up easily once he made up his mind!

During the Spring of 1940 various other defences were being set up across England to hinder invading German forces. Strategically placed pillboxes for monitoring hostile activity were sited   alongside main roads likely to be used by the enemy. Now of historical interest some of the one hundred deployed in the area around Chelmsford still remain and others exist elsewhere. Their narrow slots were for observation and the use of light weaponry if necessary. Fortified Martello towers built for use during the Napoleonic Wars were to be used for observation purposes and were particularly useful during bombing sorties by the Luftwaffe. The tower built in 1806 at Point Clear St. Osyth on the Essex Colne estuary opposite Brightlingsea is now the museum of the 'East Essex Aviation Society' housing wartime exhibits. It was a WRNS [Women's Royal Navy Service] shore base during WWII named 'HMS Helder'. The views from the top of the tower were ideal for plane spotting and shipping activity. Also the two hundred torpedo heads, buried in the estuary between there and Mersea Island, could have been detonated from the Tower.

Martello Tower, 23 Point Clear.

Pillbox.

We now know about the 'Secret Army' trained to carry out acts of sabotage if we were threatened with invasion. Their operational bases located fifteen feet underground were generally in woodland areas with suitable vegetation for disguising the entrances. With room for six to eight people they contained enough food and water and sabotage equipment to last about a fortnight, which was their expected survival rate. They were to leave home without revealing anything to their families, the prospect of which must have been challenging. In the early 1950's during trench excavations in Danbury for electricity cabling, Dad who was working in 'Public Relations' with the Eastern Electricity Board, told us about the unearthing of a dugout. He said it was well constructed with timber lining and wondered about its use. A scooped out hollow is all that remains of one near the edge of a wood in Little Baddow.

Meanwhile, three-mile zone limits were set up in the areas around London to restrict movement except for necessary travelling to school or work. Romford was on the boundary of Dagenham, which was in the City of London "Group Seven". The zoning was implemented to deter people with ulterior motives from moving around easily. Camouflage too was carried out at strategic sites like gun emplacements, runways at aerodromes and included Churchill's retreat at Chartwell in Kent to conceal the house and fishponds. Concrete blocks named "Dragons Teeth" were set up on beaches around the coasts with coiled barbed wire along the beachheads. I remember the ones at Watchet, Blue Anchor and Minehead. Immediately post-war they were to be useful 'storage heaters' for warming our towels before a swim and drying them and our costumes after.

'Starfish' decoy methods set up to confuse German aircraft included dummy planes, dumps and phoney landing lights simulating airfields. Sited on farmland with AA guns and searchlights in the vicinity, they effectively diverted bombers from their intended targets not far away. South Weald Park in the Green Belt near Brentwood was one of the locations and a field in Little Baddow near Chelmsford was used to lure the Luftwaffe away from the Hoffman and Marconi factories. In Great Baddow at the end of Molrams Lane a concrete bunker housing an 'ack ack' gun was disguised as a shop. Dummy wooden submarines, manufactured at Wivenhoe Shipyard and placed along the coast in the area of Harwich, Brightlingsea and Walton-on-Naze, were convincing enough to receive a raid from the Luftwaffe. In various open areas mock-up buildings were set up by film crews. Fires were created by the dropping of a diesel/water mix from storage tanks above preheated cast iron troughs, which blazed when detonated. Fuel supplies for our aircraft and ground force vehicles increased when a pipeline was laid from Bologne to the Kent coast. Named "PLUTO", "Pipeline under the Ocean", its terminals at Dungeness were concealed under mock buildings including a chapel.

Under a cloak of secrecy, 'Radio Location' had also been developed: sited on a sand and shingle spit at Bawdsey on a quiet part of the Suffolk coast between Felixstowe and Shingle Street. Invented by Robert Watson-Watt it had already been used by the Air Ministry in WWI but abandoned in the 1930's. Exercises carried out in 1936/37 at Biggin Hill and test flights from Martlesham meant the system was operational in advance of German air attacks. By 1940 masts had been positioned from the east coast of Scotland southwards to the Thames, around to Ventnor and westwards as far as Prestatyn in North Wales; the highest concentration being from Bawdsey to Pevensey in Sussex. The system was to be named RADAR by the Americans ('Radio And Detection And Range'. By 1945 they had contributed many more until one hundred and seventy stations covered the entire British coastline including The Hebrides off north-west Scotland. During the Blitz it was to be invaluable for RAF Fighter Command who were able to delay scrambling until enemy aircraft had been located. This saved fuel and the early warnings enabled civilians to take shelter in reasonable time. One of the masts, originally sited at Canewdon near Southend, was to be brought by Marconi's to Great Baddow in the 1950's for further development. Its height of around 360 ft. makes it visible from some distance and it is a constant reminder of how much we owe them.

Radar Mast

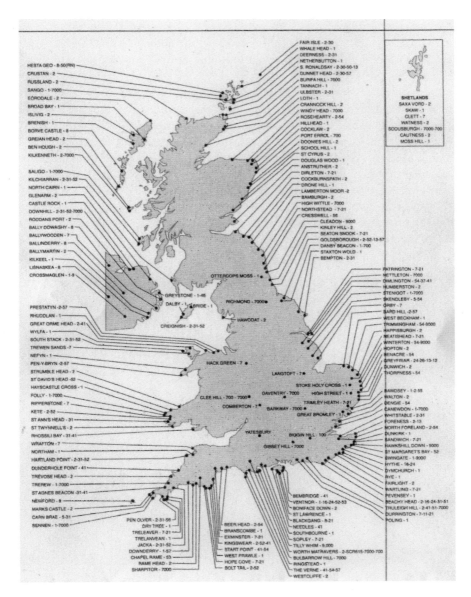

The Germans admitted at the end of the War that they hadn't, initially, anything to compare. They had been keen to find out as much as they could about our system and in the 1960'S an ex RAF pilot, whose Beaufighter had been fitted with the equipment in its fuselage, told Michael about his experiences following a night patrol over the English Channel when bad weather had hampered navigation. Identifying the Seine as the Thames he set course for Hornchurch and was given the correct signal for landing on his approach. Fired on as he came in he managed to land and was enlightened by French voices in the dark as he set off to seek help. Taken prisoner by the Germans he was subjected to a three day cycle of interrogation by the Gestapo regarding the Radar equipment. They were nice the first day, aggressive the next and ignored him on the third. He managed to programme himself in advance to this sequence but admitted a change would have made him submit. Finally released from interrogation he was marched towards the Eastern front, abandoned in a forest as the Allies approached and then had to subsist on what he could find amongst the sparse vegetation. He said, however, he had been treated better by the German prison guards than the Russians who eventually picked him up. The experience was to cause bouts of deep depression and when he finally got home he would sit in his garden shed with an axe across his knees, which he would have used if he felt threatened.

Magnetic mine, Maldon

The multitude of magnetic mines, laid by the Germans during the early months of the war, was to become a great threat to our shipping. One, which drifted ashore at Shoeburyness Essex in November '39, was dealt with successfully by a Naval Officer, and scientists were then able to produce methods for dealing with them. The 'Combined Military Service Museum' at Maldon exhibits some of ours. Varying in size they were laid in our coastal waters and estuaries during the war to protect shipping from

German U-Boats. Post-war they were to be adapted and deployed for the collection of money for charities in car parks at seaside coastal resorts. At Brightlingsea Essex near the harbour they had a small one which I believe was removed for "health and safety" reasons, but the one on the front at Burnham-on-Crouch is in a better position.

CMSM & Burnham

After we returned from Somerset in the Spring of 1940 our next priority was the installation of our underground shelter at the top of the garden. Designed in 1938 by William Paterson and Oscar Kerrison, it was named after Sir John Anderson who had become Home Secretary. Dad opted for this one as he thought it would be safer. In the event this proved to be correct for most close encounters but unfortunately not direct hits. They cost about £7-£8 with payments being means tested. One still in situ in Great Baddow in the grounds of a local undertaker is now hidden completely by foliage. Essex clay a few inches down had made our digging difficult, but mum took her turn when dad was at work. The excavation measured 6'6" x 4'6" with a depth of 4'0". The corrugated curved iron side panels were lowered in and bolted together. The floor was cemented and had a scooped out sump at the entrance for baling out, which was to become necessary early in the winter. The inner walls were lined with concrete to ground level, the recesses providing support for the upper bunk frames. Finally the curved ceiling was painted blue to simulate the sky. Near the blast wall at the entrance were sandbags, stirrup pump and three buckets: one with sand, one with water and a lidded one for slops. The exterior was then covered with the excavated clay to the recommended depth of 15" and I think eventually we managed to grow a few plants. We had to duck when entering through the front entrance, but fortunately were to be spared having to use the bolted rear emergency escape panel. They were to be very effective except for the poor people who were visibly uninjured but had the air sucked out of their lungs by the blast.

Pennack's

Jeanne & I at our shelter

A later outdoor shelter the "Appleby Dumpling" was designed and named after Romford Borough Surveyor Mr. Appleby. It looked like a giant inverted concrete pudding basin. The indoor "Morrison" named after Home Secretary Herbert Morrison was dual purpose: measuring 6ft.6" x

4ft.0" x 2ft.9" high, its caged sides and stout wooden top making it useful as a table and was designed to accommodate two adults and two small children or three adults lying down. Michael's aunt Kitty and family sheltered in the cellar of their house in Manor Park. Our friend Ron Bond remembers their black cat producing her kittens in the coal heap in the corner of theirs in Ilford: a safe and well camouflaged spot! Many people in high-density housing were less fortunate and resorted to the Underground Tube stations for shelter during raids. Initially discouraged by local authorities, for "Health and safety" reasons, eventually it became routine procedure. A TV programme revealed that during the Blitz 60,000 people sheltered in them. They soon set up forms of entertainment to help pass the time and to keep up their spirits and morale: some managing to manoeuvre pianos below.

Appleby Dumpling

Michael's Aunt, Doris Herniman, wrote brief details of the conditions at that time. "I think the saddest part of the war, apart from the heavy casualties, was seeing mothers and young children, particularly the babies, going down to the Tube platforms at 5 pm when I travelled on the Piccadilly Line from Holborn to North Southgate. They put blankets on the platform to lay on and the trains kept stopping for passengers to alight. The air in the Tubes was not pleasant and I felt very upset about this." This referred to inadequate toilet facilities, which must have presented problems with the non-disposable nappies of that time. Recently we were told by a fellow bus passenger that she had to live in the Underground when they were bombed out in Hackney as they had nowhere else to go. Keeping clean bothered her as they were only provided with a cup of water for the purpose. The young mums too must have been anxious about the safety of their young children during the rush hour as the current wasn't cut off until the trains stopped running.

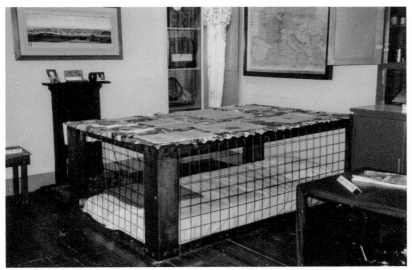

Morrison

On 11th January 1941 one hundred people were to be killed at the Bank station, many of whom I believe had attended a function nearby. The greatest tragedy was to be at Bethnall Green on 3rd March 1943. Although no alert had been sounded, the simultaneous firing of all the guns in a practise session in Victoria Park caused panic because, for security reasons, no prior notice had been given to the public. The deafening noise, interpreted as bombs, precipitated a dash for the safety of the Underground and a young girl tripping near the bottom of the entrance steps caused an unstoppable wave of panic stricken people to pile on top of her. One hundred and seventy were killed and Press reports at the time blamed the public, but many years later the real truth was to be revealed. I believe there is a plaque somewhere in the vicinity, which records the tragic event.

In Romford our nearest siren was at Collier Row Police Station. An above ground public shelter and first-aid hut were positioned at the rear of the Parkside Hotel, now named "The Squire", and fire watching points were established in various places. On a visit to the Amberley Museum near Arundel we spotted a 'one man' shelter or observer post?

An observer box at the Amberley Museum

Black on the outside and with a white interior it had a grab handle to close the door, a perch to sit on and a ledge for recording notes of incidents. Our brick built wardens' post was set up at the North Street end of Parkside Avenue and on our return from evacuation in Somerset our nearest warden Mr. Jeffery who lived opposite us kitted us out with gasmasks. Apparently these had been available as early as 1938. Jeanne and I had the childrens' size, and toddlers' masks had Mickey Mouse ears. The one for babies had fastenings at the crutch to facilitate nappy changing and had an air pump attachment. A gas proof box for dogs was provided by the PDSA costing £4, which was quite an expense in those days and I imagine it must have been difficult to persuade one into it. Apparently they were banned from public shelters which maybe explains why many were put down before the Blitz started. Also, with rationing, it wasn't easy to provide them with enough food.

Masks: Child - Gt.Yarmouth, and Adult – Glen Opie's museum

In our masks we looked like truncated baby elephants or TV 'Teletubbies': the rubber masks were stuffy, the visor soon misted up and conversation for a chatterbox wouldn't have been easy! Metal cylinders were to replace our battered boxes and the more fashion conscious grown-ups chose zipped leatherette cases. Until the threat receded we carried ours everywhere.

CMSM Maldon - baby

The primitive warning of a gas attack was a painted wooden square on a post, which would change colour if one occurred. I checked the one in the front garden of the Turnbull's house every time I passed it. We now know that in 1940 smoke bombs and mustard gas were being produced secretly in Flintshire North Wales and I'm so glad that neither side used them. Later, apparently, anthrax was also to be contemplated and I thank God that the use of this never materialised.

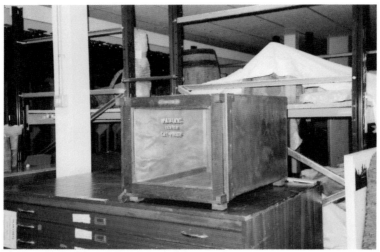

A Dog Box (Essex Regiment Museum)

For our blackout we had wooden frames with thick material tacked on which were attached to anchor points around our downstairs windows and upstairs the curtains were pulled over with precision and dim torches used carefully if necessary. These measures proved to be effective and I don't remember any wardens shouting out "Put that light out" in our immediate vicinity. It took some time for people to get used to the blackout and during December 1939 nearly 1,200 had been killed in accidents before bombing commenced. When we had to go out in the dark we soon recognised the shapes of the hedges and gates of various neighbours and, with the restricted light of our torches, knew when to turn in at our own.

Although not obligatory, Jeanne and I had identity discs. It was important as we were no longer living in the zone in which we had been registered and the address was important. Mum and Dad's registrations were DCJK/190/1 & 2. Engraved with our Somerset number and Romford address, we wore our discs around our necks and I still have mine. Mum mentioned that she would recognise me by the mole on the underside of my left foot. Sadly, when hostilities began, several unfortunate victims were to be buried in Romford Cemetery with the inscription 'Known only to God.'

Aunt Phyl recalled a night in 1940 in Somerset when she and Uncle Ray were walking home to Watchet after visiting Gran and Grandad at Timberscombe. Just before Dunster two dim figures emerged from a hedge demanding their identity cards and, as they were without them, she had to present them next morning at Watchet Council Office. The issue of identity cards was to continue until after the War was over.

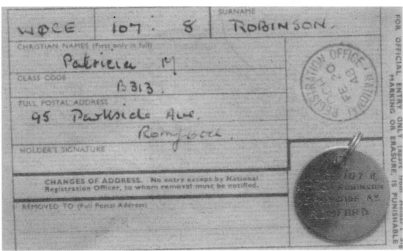

My card and identity disc

Petrol had been rationed on September 16th 1939 with supplies limited. "Pool" petrol was introduced costing 1/6d. a gallon rising to just over 2/-d. Eventually only people with legitimate reasons had an allowance and this was to continue until 1945. To prevent their use in the event of occupation the rotor arms of non-essential vehicles were handed in to Romford Police Station and I remember collecting ours at the end of the War. Covered with dust sheets our Jowett was jacked up to help preserve her tyres and at regular intervals pushed out onto the drive and back. She was Dad's pride and joy and we missed our outings in her. Our next door neighbour Mr. Brown, who had a limousine, had to give up chauffeuring and moved to Manor Park where he had a newsagent and tobacconist shop in the Broadway. Jeanne and I made regular checks of their house until finally it was sold. Walking soon became routine and many people joined the 'Bicycle Brigade'. It helped to keep us fit too and Dad and I occasionally cycled to Manor Park to see the Brown family.

After Anthony Eden's appeal for Local Defence Volunteers in May

1940, Romford men came forward to offer their services and took part in a march in their 'Civvies' through the Market. In July they were to be renamed the Home Guard. Dad hadn't been called up to join the Forces as he was in a 'Reserved Occupation', working on a shift system in Romford's substation which supplied electricity to a wide area. He registered with the London Electricity Supply Company '1st Essex (Ind.) Company' on 7th August 1940. They had regular training sessions and in August received their rifles. When asked by their instructor "what is the first thing you do before cleaning your gun", Dad with his impish sense of humour replied "Make sure it's your own"! He had been enlisted in the 17th London Rifle Brigade in 1917 and knew only too well how to use one. He blotted his copybook also by naming the machine gun and grenades 'Lewis' and 'Mills' and I can picture him being given a Captain Mainwaring stare!

Dad's Identity Card

Although Dad didn't say much about his activities he told cousin Don Wilson that he got very tired when practising setting up tank traps. Made from lengths of railway line bent into a "V" shape they were lowered into holes in the road as obstacles. He wasn't tall and it must have been a tremendous effort. After sessions he walked home and I'd listen for the sound of his boots before settling to sleep. One night I was physically sick with worry when he didn't get home until very late. He must have been so tired and, when he slept before and after night shifts at the substation, Jeanne and I crept around the house and avoided the second step of the stairs which creaked: I wonder if it still does? The Home Guard was to be disbanded in 1944.

March through Romford

Many years later Dad was to recall some of his experiences during WWI and we still have several of his basic necessities for his time in the trenches including his dog tag with identity number and the New Testament with the signature of his Padre. He was in France by Aug. 1917 after three months training on the Isle of Sheppey in Kent. We have the mouthpiece of his bugle and TV programmes have since revealed some of the horrors he must have experienced as we learned that buglers were assigned as stretcher-bearers. He was in the 17th London Rifle Brigade and by the time he got to France was probably involved in the third Battle of Ypres in July 1917. He brought home a souvenir brass ashtray with an engraving of the Menin Gate at Ypres and I remember him always removing his hat and standing with head bowed when funeral processions passed by. During that time Mum had been an inspector of shells in a Coventry munitions factory. I feel sorry for the people of their generation: they experienced WWI, brought us up in our early years during the 'Depression' and then had to face WWII only twenty-one years after the first one. I remember Mum saying "Be a brave soldier" when I had nasty tumbles when very young: a saying which probably originated from that time.

During the week commencing May 26th 1940 after the capitulation of the French, the subsequent rescue of the British Expeditionary Force from the Dunkirk beaches, codenamed 'Dynamo', is something we will never forget. With sheer guts and determination all manner of ships numbering over 800 took part in the memorable rescue, fiercely protected by Naval gunfire and limited RAF planes overhead. Boat owning Brits. from the south and east coasts puttered or chugged and others were tugged or sailed across the Channel in the massive operation. Many of them made several journeys and we still remember the film 'Mrs. Miniver', starring Greer Garson and Walter Pigeon and later 'Snow Goose' starring Richard Harris and Jenny Agutter.

Sailing Barge Pudge

Amongst the Thames Sailing Barges who took part in the evacuation was 'Pudge' who is usually moored at Maldon. Built in 1922 and fitted with an auxiliary engine in 1930, her large deck space, roomy hold and a draught of 3'6" made her ideal for getting close to the Dunkirk beaches. Her crew of two were awaiting an assignment of cargo at Tilbury at the end of May 1940 when she was enlisted and sent to Dover. Lots had to be drawn as so many skippers volunteered. As one of the 'Little Ships' she was to bring back a total of around 300 men. For fuel economy she and barges 'Thrya' and 'Lady Rosebery' were towed in the darkness by tug

'St. Fagan` who, having cast off, hit a mine with only six of her crew surviving. 'Pudge` settled right way up, picked up the six 'Fagan` survivors plus those from other barges and then troops from the beaches. She was towed for the latter part of the three hour return journey to Ramsgate by another tug 'Tanga'. Eighteen of the participating Essex barges survived, but unfortunately twelve were lost as they were easy targets for the Luftwaffe. 'Pudge' was to be bought by the Thames Barge Sailing Club in 1968, refitted and rigged to original design and now runs Charter trips from Maldon in Essex for Club members. She crossed to France in 1990 for the fiftieth anniversary of Dunkirk and in May 2010 at Ipswich Dock we were among the crowd who were allowed to board her for the seventieth.

We have also been told how a serving Kentish fisherman, marooned on the French coast with a wounded colleague, searched until he found a boat. Conversant with tides, currents and weather conditions in the Channel made him determined to get them both back home and he rowed the boat across to St. Margarets Bay on the Kent coast. Able-bodied men were expected to get back to England to fight again and were also anxious to see their families. Ernie Othen a near neighbour in great Baddow was in the Medical Corps. Hotly pursued to the coast he and his colleagues jettisoned equipment from their lorry, abandoned it and joined a crocodile to await rescue from the ships off shore. The queues were strafed by the Luftwaffe, but he managed finally to shin up a rope to board a ship. He told us that for reasons of public morale, when they reached England they were not allowed to disembark until nightfall so that local citizens couldn't witness the pitiful condition of some of them. They were given blankets and cups of tea by the WVS ['Women's Voluntary Services']. The combined efforts of all the courageous boats and crews who took part were to bring back to England around 338,000 troops and 39,000 French soldiers, many of whom had mounted a rearguard action during the final evacuation on 3rd June. The total was about seven times the number anticipated. On 4th June Winston Churchill gave details in the House of Commons of the 'Miracle of Dunkirk'. On Thursday May 30th, during the period of the evacuation, the Minister of Transport Sir John Reith ordered the removal of signposts from areas likely to be involved in an invasion. With our car out of action and knowing our immediate area well this was no problem for us.

On June 22nd 1940 a Franco-German Armistice was signed. Terrible decisions have to be made during times of War and the French reacted badly when Churchill gave instructions for their Fleet to be destroyed to prevent its use by the Germans. Tragically 1,200 Frenchmen were killed. It was during this month whilst awaiting a possible invasion that

Churchill arranged the setting up of the 1st Division of Paratroopers. They were to be fighting in North Africa in May 1943 and later in Normandy in 1944.

July 10th 1940 is the date considered to be the beginning of the Battle of Britain and on the 16th Hitler threatened his invasion, Operation Sealion, by 15th August. The Royal British Legion record that at that time only 2,927 RAF members were available. It was in July that Lord Beaverbrook announced a national appeal for aluminium salvage for the manufacture of Spitfire and Hurricane fighters and Blenheim and Wellington bombers: these costing £6,000, £4,500, £317,000 and £25,000 respectively. Fighter Command's 640 fighters were far outnumbered by the Luftwaffe 2,600 bombers and fighters. The daylight raids were to continue until early September and many areas in England were affected with the South coast, Kent and Essex being major targets.

Spitfire fighter fund poster

In June 2011, we visited the 'Battle of Britain' Memorial sited on the cliff top at Capel le Ferne in Kent. The statue of a young pilot, sitting and gazing out to sea, was unveiled by HM Queen Elizabeth the Queen Mother on 9th July 1993. Carved along the base of a memorial wall nearby are the words of Winston Churchill "Never in the field of human conflict was so much owed by so many to so few" and the memorial wall lists nearly 3,000 names of the aircrews from many countries who participated, including the survivors. A replica Spitfire and Hurricane stand near the visitor centre.

Memorial Wall

During the Battle period we had been so grateful for the valiant efforts of the pilots who tackled the Luftwaffe and soon recognised the comforting sound of the Spitfires. Squadrons 54, 65, 74 and 41 operated from Romford's nearest RAF base at Hornchurch. It was a strategic target and only about three miles away from us as the crow flies. Other bases in Essex were at North Weald, Debden, Stapleford Abbots and Rochford from which flew, variously, Spitfires, Hurricanes and Blenheims. We have witnessed some Battle of Britain memorial flights when they have passed over Great Baddow on their way to London and the sound of the Spitfire is unmistakeable.

Memorial Flight

Cousin Geoffrey Prole who lived at Brasted near Biggin Hill in Kent remembers the raids well as the RAF fighter station there was also a prime target. Uncle George was a gamekeeper for Lord Stanhope at Chevening and a large communal shelter was built for the estate staff. Geoffrey has told us that an Old English sheepdog belonging to a member of staff reacted immediately the siren went and was always first to the shelter where he sat obediently with the handbag of his mistress in his mouth. It couldn't have been easy for the people living in that area as Churchill's home at Chartwell wasn't far away and the Luftwaffe were seeking that as well as Biggin Hill. I remember Aunt Amy recalling how she was so terrified one day that she climbed a tree in the orchard. She decided to take Geoffrey down to Somerset to live with her sister near Wheddon Cross and he remembers sleeping overnight with the crowds in the underground at Paddington Station. Aunt Amy returned to Kent the following day.

On Saturday 29 July 1940 Hitler threatened Britain by announcing "Talk peace or I destroy you". A meticulous record of incidents in the Romford area appears in Peter Watt's 'Hitler v. Havering', the first incident occurring during the afternoon of 1st August when incendiaries landed on Harold Wood station. On 20th August, not long before my ninth birthday, we all listened to Churchill's legendary speech "We shall go on to the end... we shall defend our island... we shall fight in the fields and in the streets.. we shall never surrender". It was scary listening and I visualised a booted and helmeted German soldier scaling a ladder to my bedroom window to get me personally! My imagination raced ahead of me as I went up to bed and I decided to keep my window shut, pull the bedclothes up tight under my chin to protect me and hoped we would all be safe.

time we had run outside to spot occasional planes but during were to run underground for shelter. During a daytime incident, d I ventured out of our Anderson shelter to witness a 'dog fight' involving two British fighters and a lone German plane proceeding eastwards to the coast; maybe on a reconnaissance run? We heard the 'rat a tat tat' of machine gunfire as one fired at its rear whilst the other went on ahead to return for a frontal attack. When a loan parachutist bailed out, Mrs. Macbeth's son-in-law Eric Dawkins pulled on his 'Home Guard' armband in readiness as the airman floated down manoeuvring his parachute and I still remember seeing clearly the underside of his flying boots as he floated across our back gardens. News was restricted but Jeanne was told by Mr. Jefferys, our warden, that local members of the Home Guard had taken an airman into custody when he landed on the then undeveloped hill at the end of Parkside Avenue. Aerial photographs of Romford, Hornchurch and Dagenham taken by the Luftwaffe in early September 1940, show clearly the railway lines, roads, housing, schools etc. When magnified, Michael and I can pick out the avenue in which we both lived and the schools we attended.

Michael's school St. Edwards at the top end of Romford market place had brick built shelters above ground. When the bombing began his elder brother Peter spent a whole term studying at home as the Mercers school at Holborn in the City was considered too dangerous. My school, then named "Havering Road" and now "Parklands", had underground shelters in the playing field with bench seating either side and duck boards to walk on as they were prone to flooding. We sang popular songs, which included "Roll out the barrel", "Ten green bottles" and "The Quartermaster's Stores". Because of the primitive curtained off loo at the entrance, the skimpy curtain and sound effects from the galvanized bucket, I'd cross my legs hoping the raid wouldn't last long! We weren't allowed home alone until the "All Clear" and an entry in the school log records one air raid lasting from 11.55 am until after 4 pm which necessitated cancelling the afternoon session for the day. This was probably an occasion when Dad fetched me home on the crossbar of his bicycle. Normally we walked home in groups and I remember two Jewish sisters Ruth and Naomi Jacobs being teased by a boy. Any hint of Anti-Semitism was not tolerated and the next morning he was summoned to the headmaster Mr. Bird's study and caned for his insensitive comments.

At Romford we were in 'bomb alley' about three quarters of the way from the mouth of the Thames to the City. Another target on the way to London was Fords at Dagenham. Our nearest was the Ack Ack 'Anti-Aircraft' gun emplacement at Whalebone Lane only two roundabouts from the end of our road. Not knowing when our area would be affected we took to the shelter each night for safety. At first I slept across the width alongside the escape panel at the rear. The spanner for this was kept in the same place for immediate retrieval in an emergency in the dark. Later I occupied the upper bunk lengthwise opposite Jeanne whilst Mum and Dad, when he was off duty, used the lower ones. My bunk was fine for me but tubby adults must have preferred sitting. The narrow gap between them left little room for manoeuvre when climbing up and down. Families of six also had to make do with seating arrangements, which must have been very tiring during long raids.

Dad had run a lead covered cable to the shelter with a fixed switchboard at the entrance, which provided us with light and we had a 12 volt auxiliary battery for use during power cuts. Because of the possibility of invasion we had an emergency supply of tinned meat, soup and fruit in an emptied tool box, but eventually it was to be moved to the garage to make more room when the raids became relentless. Michael's family had a surface Anderson with a reinforced concrete covering of fifteen inches. Condensation was to be a problem in both shelters and Michael awoke each morning with cork chippings in his hair from the coated walls! It is recorded that on the first night of the Blitz when the Docks were targeted, 600 bombers along with 600 fighter escorts took part. On this and subsequent nights a ribbon of fires guided later bombers to their targets and ex Luftwaffe pilots have since admitted that, if the City was well alight on their final approach, they would tip their bombs out on the suburbs for a quick getaway which explains why Romford and surrounding districts were victims.

Searchlights probed the sky like laser beams in their search for enemy planes and on one occasion as we hurried to the shelter I had a quick glimpse of a barrage balloon at the Whalebone Ack Ack gun site being lit up. They resembled enormous grey whales with three inflated fins at the rear for balance. Barges in line across the Thames from Southend to Sheerness in Kent, with a balloon apiece aloft, were an attempt to deter low flying German bombers. The menace from the sky today is the pollution from criss-crossing vapour trails of airliners making their way to and from Heathrow and Stansted. BBC news bulletins during the Blitz bombardment revealed nothing regarding locations because of security. Word of mouth information and the "I Spy Stranger" slogan stirred imaginations and paranoia set in when a neighbour reported having seen a person in a white coat flashing a torch into the sky perhaps to direct planes. It was probably an air raid warden checking someone's blackout.

In the summer of 1940 anti-aircraft batteries had been established at Bedfords Park at Havering, which had been a favourite picnic spot for us pre-war. From there Dad had pointed out various things silhouetted against the skyline including St. Pauls and across the Thames to Shooters Hill in Kent. The Mansion, which has since been demolished, was a good vantage point for monitoring the severity of fires in the City and Mr. Bowles of Little Baddow who served with the AFS (Auxiliary Fire Service) told us that it only took about thirty minutes to get to the hotspots. Fire crews from all around London were on constant call and must have been very busy. Miraculously St. Pauls survived and now the subsequent redevelopment of the City can be seen clearly from the viewpoint in front of the Visitor Centre.

It was after the bombing of Berlin that Hitler had retaliated by ordering the Luftwaffe to target the City of London and the night-time BLITZ in our area began in the early morning of 9th September, my 9th birthday, when an HE (High Explosive) dropped at 35 Parkside Avenue: we lived at 95. We were to receive a selection of bombs, all equally lethal. The incendiaries were in a massive container shell and caused a lot of damage. The high explosives varied in weight. On 23rd September 1940 an unexploded parachute mine at Birkbeck Road was to be taken to Bedfords Park to be dealt with by a Bomb Disposal unit. The last time we paid a visit it was good to see the park still has deer and to remember the happy times we spent there when young.

Incendiary Basket

Early on in the Blitz it was therapeutic to have things to do in the shelter. On scraps of paper we played 'Hangman', 'Battleships' and 'Noughts and Crosses'. Also 'Catscradle' with wool looped across our fingers. I made bracelets from stripped and discarded coloured flex, also a multi-coloured snake with a cotton reel with four nails on the top, a crochet hook and coloured wool remnants. Miniature knitted dolls I stuffed into my handkerchief sachet dog. I always took him with me to the shelter. Anxious that we might be separated, I put his name and our address inside him. He was to accompany me once more when I returned to Somerset in July 1944. 'I Spy' objects became repetitive in the confines of the shelter and 'Bunks, blankets, buckets and bolts' were soon joined by 'beetles' when the floor became waterlogged.

High Explosive bombs

Someone recalled suffering with severe earache and her doctor removing a beetle from it the following morning. 'Creepy crawlies' weren't the only things to bother us. An escapee newt from next door's flooded pond, in search of a 'bosom friend', plummeted onto mum's bare flesh. The next morning the 'offending corpse' was lying alongside the escape panel spanner! Only recently, I was told by a shopper that they had rats in their shelter and I don't know how we would have coped with that. With the culling of so many domestic cats earlier on, rats were to become a health hazard as the war progressed and, during the final year, around four million of them were to be eliminated.

The night a particularly close bomb came whistling down Jeanne and I rolled simultaneously out of the top bunks and landed in a heap of blankets on the floor. It damaged the rear of a house in Eastern Avenue whose back garden adjoined Michael's at number 57 Parkside. When we came out from our shelter we could see tattered curtains flapping through shattered windows and the shelves of an exposed airing cupboard revealing a chamber pot on one and neat rows of bottled fruit and preserves on others. The shattered rear wall of the house was to be rebuilt in due course. The explosion had blown Michael out of his top bunk and,

59

after enquiring "was that a bomb", he fell asleep immediately and had to be shovelled back into his bunk! I found it more difficult and would come out of the shelter in the morning rubbing the sleep out of my eyes and trying to adjust to the daylight. Michael's grandfather Lambert described tired eyes as "Burnt holes in a blanket" and I know exactly what he meant. Desperate for sleep we still had to go to school and get on with life.

We felt particularly vulnerable on moonlit nights as we were in the Luftwaffe's bombing corridor to the City from the coast. One route was the A127 arterial road at the back of us, another the main railway line to Liverpool Street with the Romford electricity substation and adjacent gasometers providing good targets on the way. To the south the glistening ribbon of the Thames guided them to Fords and the Docks. They dropped HE's (High Explosives), incendiaries, oil bombs, and parachute mines: the last being a 'misnomer' as they were a different shape and were dropped and not buried like conventional mines. Six or eight feet in length they were carried in pairs with one suspended beneath each wing of the bomber and landing in close proximity to one another. Floating down silently until a device released them, their final swish and explosion on impact was terrifying and they were the ones that frightened me most. I discovered a wealth of information concerning incidents that affected us from Dad's original copy of *Ordeal in Romford* and a meticulous recorded account from Peter Watt's book *Hitler v. Havering*.

Coastal areas had been amongst the first to suffer from bombing and leaflets containing Hitler's 'Last Appeal to Reason', translated from his speech to the Reichstag the previous month had been dropped in August admonishing our leaders for lack of peace negotiations. The City had suffered on 9th September and a newspaper in 1948 recorded how, nearby to St. Pauls, a cat called Faith had protected her kitten in the rectory of St. Augustine by Faith whilst it blazed and floors collapsed. Later she was to be awarded three certificates for her bravery and courage. In Romford on the night of the 10th there were nine incidents beginning with an HE at North Street's junction with Eastern Avenue near the top of Parkside. Bombardment ceased at 04.23 am and later at 20.15 pm there were fifteen more including the destruction by an HE of a house not far from us in the vicinity of Hill Grove and Cedric Avenue. A picture of this incident in the archives of Havering Local Studies Library, showing an upended bath, demonstrates the peril of taking one during a raid.

Damage to 40 Cedric Avenue

The survival of St. Paul's cathedral was to be a great morale booster to all Londoners. A delayed action bomb, buried 27 ft. down in Deans Yard on September 12th 1940, took three days to dig up. It was taken by lorry to Hackney Marshes where it was blown up causing a 100 ft. crater. The team leader Lt. Davies was to be awarded the first George Medal. In the grounds of the Cathedral there is a memorial to the Fire Fighters who fought so bravely to protect and rescue people during the Blitz. Unveiled by HM the Queen Mother on 4th May 1991, it was re-dedicated and unveiled by HRH The Princess Royal on 4th May 2003. At the beginning of 1940 some firemen volunteers had been dubbed unfairly by some as 'army dodgers' but, for their unstinting efforts, Winston Churchill was to call them 'heroes with grimy faces'. They were compassionate men and our neighbour Doris Hill has told us how her father, a member of the AFS (Auxiliary Fire Service), would return home mentally and physically exhausted, his eyes circled with soot, lids burned away and brows and hairline singed. He'd sit with his head in his hands crying about his experiences, which upset all of them. They lived in Finsbury Park and a bomb, dropping nearby, blew in all their windows and toppled furniture. It killed the mother of Doris' friend whose father was away on Service. Doris' father who attended the incident didn't get home for three days.

The nightly raids were to be relentless and I remember quite clearly our close encounters. On 20th September at 23.50 pm two houses were demolished by an HE in Havering Drive causing four fatalities. On 5th October 1940 another three dropped nearby: an unexploded one at the junction of Eastern Avenue and Ashmour Gardens at the back of us and another which demolished three houses in Pammer Avenue (this is now the continuation of Parkside Avenue to Pettits Lane). A third fell on a bungalow a short distance away from us in Fontayne Avenue trapping a mother and two daughters. As the firemen were unable to reach them, their small father located them and assisted in their rescue. On October 10th an HE demolished a house in nearby Eastern Avenue killing one person and a second exploded in Ashmour Gardens demolishing two houses near the entry I used at the rear of Havering Road (now 'Parklands') School.

As time progressed we got colder in the shelter in spite of the layers of clothes we wore and we were having to bail out the sump more frequently: [1940 was to be recorded as the coldest winter for forty years.] Like many others we decided to return to our beds indoors. Jeanne and Mum were always the first to go downstairs when the alert sounded and sometimes I'd wait until I could hear Dad getting up and the unmistakeable sound of the Junkers 88 bombers overhead. The first thing we did was to put on the kettle for a 'comforting cuppa'. When Dad was off night duty at the substation during heavy raids he escorted us in turn to the shelter with his Home Guard helmet over our heads. Apparently more people were killed by shrapnel from the 'Ack Ack' guns than by the bombing. Our largest piece spun down and shredded a cabbage in our vegetable patch. It was chunky, jagged and about 6" long and was still warm when we picked it up the next morning. Initially Dad had thought the damage had been done by a cabbage white butterfly! The cabbage was of little use but at least we had been spared. The morning after heavy raids we'd pick up pieces from the pavements on the way to school.

Air Raid Siren

Junkers 88

On the night of 13th October 1940 Haysoms furniture store on the corner of Church Lane and North Street was set alight along with the almshouses opposite. The brewery was also hit and, on returning to bed after the 'All Clear', I could see from my front bedroom window the spectacular but sinister bright orange and yellow flames leaping high into the angry red night sky with the top layer black: ironically the three colours of the German flag. The blaze was to continue well into the early hours. [Haysoms` levelled site was to be left like so many others for the duration of the War.]

Haysoms, the morning after

Romford Market - Savings Bonds

The mornings after raids the air was still acrid from the smoke which had drifted across: a bit like the aftermath of fireworks and bonfires on 'Guy Fawkes' night.. Shopkeepers swept up the broken glass, boarded up their windows and painted across them 'Business as Usual'. Cousin Don Wilson remarked that it saved his daily chore of cleaning the shop windows at 'Adams' the Ironmongers in the Market Place. The picture of the Market shows their blocked windows and letters missing from their facade and also the adjacent Midland Bank's slogan 'Buy Savings Bonds'

During the moonlit night of 15/16th October 1940 there were thirty-seven incidents over a wide area. High Explosives predominated and there were also Parachute Mines and Incendiaries. Twenty-one houses were demolished with ten fatalities and six wounded being recorded. Because raids persisted, a double bed was brought down to our sitting room and put on chocks, with Mum and Dad sleeping on top and Jeanne and I on a mattress beneath. Many people had to be found temporary accommodation when their homes had been badly damaged or for other reasons. Cousin Ray Robinson and pet dog Billy stayed with us whilst fifteen unexploded bombs, dropped on 3rd November in the Lingfield Avenue Upminster area, were de-fused. The weather was appalling at the time and Billy had to be rubbed down vigorously after his evening walks.

Pets were a great comfort during the war and pilots had them as mascots, but it must have been devastating for them when crew members failed to return. After bombing incidents confused dogs would run frantically around looking for their owners buried under the rubble of what had been their homes. Those rounded up, who no longer had homes to go to, were used to find trapped survivors. A mongrel terrier in East London joined the local Civil Defence and was of great assistance as a sniffer rescue dog. Having assisted in the rescue of over one hundred he was to be awarded a PDSA 'Dickin Medal' and was buried eventually in 1946 at Ilford's animal cemetery. His epitaph reads 'RIP.D.M'; "We also serve - for the dog whose body lies here played his part in the Battle of Britain". Many had been put down at the beginning of the War to save potential distress and vets were kept busy. Sadly, they weren't allowed in the Underground and this must have been very upsetting for their owners.

During their journey home from evacuation in Oare in Wiltshire with their mother, Michael and Peter had been told by their father that Brutus their bulldog had been put to sleep the day after War was declared. He was already suffering from eczema and had to be left alone most of the day whilst their father was at work. Brutus had been trained to let people in and out of the house on command and it would have been difficult for rescuers to gain entry if they were trapped in debris. I think it is probably why Michael has never wanted to have a pet as he felt it was a betrayal as Brutus had no choice in the matter.

Meanwhile, our sleeping arrangements downstairs had continued during the winter until the morning I couldn't resist pushing out the chock nearest me which had shifted. The bed lurched and mum was not amused! It was returned upstairs and, as they were the safest place, we then slept in the cupboards under the stairs. Whilst clearing them out I spotted a German helmet badge from WWI and, being weary of the nightly attacks and probably influenced by anti-German propaganda, I asked Dad if he had killed any Germans. He was kind and gentle, bless him, and his memories of the trenches in 1917 when he was only eighteen must still have been with him. He was so upset he didn't answer me and I have never forgiven myself for asking him. Jeanne and I crammed into the sloping cupboard where I slept next to the meter boxes with Jeanne curved around me. I tried to avoid hitting my head on them when we synchronised turning over. Mum was in the adjoining cupboard under the landing with her legs sticking out in the hall. Because we were so uncomfortable a double mattress was brought down to the dining room and we all slept across the width. Each night the blackout was put up, furniture moved to accommodate the mattress, pictures taken off the wall and nearby ornaments removed. Finally the fire was damped down and a guard put in front. The next morning the mattress was rolled up and everything else was done in reverse! It was a very difficult time but Mum coped well: the only time I remember her crying was when two precious boiled eggs for our tea smashed when she tripped on the carpet. Eggs were so scarce that occasionally adults only had about one a month. She had sacrificed hers for us and I'm sure she went without many times so that we could have more to eat.

On 13th November 1940 five HE's dropped on our area just before 9 p.m. landing in Ashmour Gardens, Eastern Avenue, North Street and on Havering Road School where the Hall was badly damaged. Fortunately it was at night and we were at home, but we couldn't use the hall for some time as house repairs had priority. This incident was reported in the school's log.

Nov. 14th 1940 - Last night at 7 pm the school was struck by two HE bombs doing considerable damage and rendering the building unfit temporarily.

Havering Road School Hall

This was also the night when Coventry suffered so badly, the Luftwaffe bombing the many factories in the area contributing to the war effort.

The cathedral was also to be a targeted along with other major cathedral cities: the Germans using their pre-war 'Baedeker` cathedral and ancient monuments guides with maps to pinpoint them. The cross at the altar end of Coventry`s gutted cathedral, fashioned from pieces of debris, is a reminder of that terrible night. Beneath the cross in gold letters are the words 'FATHER FORGIVE' and below a 'Litany of Reconciliation`. The Coventry cinema, which at that time was featuring the film 'Gone with the Wind`, was wrecked and people commented on the appropriate title. The film was the first to have an interval halfway through and at Romford I remember the long queue at the 'Ritz`. Cinema going was a form of escapism where we could forget the outside world and I remember Scarlet O'Hara's words "I'll think about it tomorrow". This is what a lot of us were endeavouring to do in order to forget the realities of war.

Gone with the Wind

On November 24th 1940, Cedric Avenue, only about half a mile from us, suffered again when a parachute mine whooshed down. A stool removed hastily for Jeanne's retreat caught me as I scrambled for cover under the table and I cried as I nursed my nose. We were very fortunate as elsewhere ten houses were destroyed, five people killed and twenty-three wounded. On 8th December yet another mine demolished two shops at the junction of Exchange Street and South Street opposite Dolcis shoe shop and the entrance to the Arcade. Two people were killed and the Telephone Exchange severely damaged. Brewery staff firewatchers kept in constant touch with the substation and contacted Dad to warn him that one was floating in his direction. The site of the two shops on the corner of Exchange Street was to be cleared and I recall the space being occupied by a greengrocer's stall. The Exchange was an obvious target and when out of action, brave Scouts and other youngsters delivered messages and telegrams to key destinations. Because of this Aunt Emmie and cousin Bernard from Coventry arrived just before Christmas on a surprise visit ahead of their telegram. No doubt they were still recovering from the bombing there on 14th November, but we had to make some hurried arrangements to accommodate them and mum hoped we would have enough rations for everyone. We were, however, spared the anxiety of receiving the telegram beforehand as people dreaded their delivery in case they brought bad news.

Exchange

Significantly there were no raids in our area on the nights of 24/25/26th December, and for us they were 'silent nights' and we slept in 'heavenly peace'. Could this have been a repetition of the Christmas in the trenches during WWI when the German and British troops ceased fire and played football? The parachute mines frightened me the most and it is recorded that Essex had received 528; 106 of which failed to explode. On the 27th, Bernard, Jeanne and I walked via Pettits Lane to view one, which had landed at the corner of Balgores Lane and Main Road. With its parachute still attached it had been cordoned off at a safe distance prior to its removal to Portsmouth by a Naval bomb disposal team. These men were 'on the top of their job literally' and I have the greatest admiration for them as they risked their lives many times and I have read that their casualty rate was amongst the highest during the War. The parachutes were sought after by enterprising stallholders in Romford Market who acquired quite a few. It was a tedious job unpicking the brown seams but they were useful for making underwear, blouses etc. Its diaphanous quality, unfortunately, revealed the underwear of a young bride whose picture appeared in a local newspaper!

South Street shops

During 1940-1941 we had a bumper crop of weddings from my mother's branch of the family tree, which unfortunately we were unable to attend because of their locations. In Somerset there were three: Aunt Phyllis & Ray Bryant, Aunt Kath & Uncle Ern Ray and Uncle Harry and Bessie Cadwallader. Aunt Phyllis wore a formal dress and the other two brides smart suits, which were popular for wartime weddings. For us the choice of gifts was difficult, as household linen required coupons and postal deliveries couldn't be guaranteed. There were weddings too amongst Michael's relations and his cousin Dorothy Lambert was married to David Capps at St. Edwards church Romford. Having waited to see the guests arriving at Dorothy's house opposite I later went to the church and peeped through the door into the dim interior to see her white dress brightening as they processed up the aisle. I then hurried out before they emerged into the sunlight for the photographs.

Brewery

Aunty Kath, Dorothy & David

Dorothy's sister Hazel was a Queen Alexandra nurse and one of her patients at a Basingstoke hospital was to be a young Naval Officer John Henderson who was Second-in-Command to Captain Peter Scott on an SGB, (steam gunboat) on patrols in the English Channel. The boat was named 'Grey Goose`: this apparently being the name of the first boat Scott had as a youngster. Kitty, the youngest of Michael's cousins who served in the WAAF (Women's Auxiliary Air Force} was to marry an RAF member Dennis Chilcott and eventually they were to convert an RAF Communications van into a motorhome which had amazing space inside. Titch Perry and Win were also married in this period. He was an oil tanker captain and, following the entry of Italy into the War in 1940, he made regular trips to Malta. He was torpedoed many times but survived. Immersion in oily waters did, however, affect his lungs.

Titch & Win

72

On 29th December St. Pauls was threatened once more and would almost certainly have been destroyed but for the vigilance and prompt action of the 'Watch'. They dealt with it all in spite of the lack of water due to a water mains fracture and, as a result, Winston Churchill's message for it to be saved was fulfilled. Jeanne and I had already given up Brownies at Mawney Road Methodist Church hall because of the blackout and, when HE's on the night of 5th January 1941 caused damage in the town centre extending to the church, we decided not to resume. We had enjoyed our sessions: Jeanne was in the 'Pixies' and I appropriately enough the 'Little People'. The nightly raids, noise and apprehension continued throughout February, March and into April 1941 and we felt guilty when we weren't affected personally knowing that other people were taking the brunt of it, particularly the night of 19th and early morning of 20th March when HE's, incendiaries and parachute mines caused much damage making it Romford's worst night and I thought it would never end.

Michael's maternal grandparents Lambert lived in Cross Road and on that night, in nearby Essex Road, a parachute mine demolished seventeen houses killing thirty-eight people including Edwin Limehouse, his wife and three of his children. His surviving daughter was out fetching a meal from the Marlborough Road fish and chip shop and it must have been a terrible shock for her when she returned home. Her father was an Electricity Company fitter and his loss meant his colleagues had to close ranks to cover the constant workload. Another mine demolished fifteen houses in Pettits Lane not far away from us. Of the total 127 casualties that night 44 of them were fatalities, 93 houses were demolished and around 2,000 damaged. It wasn't an easy time for the rescue squads, fire and medical services and the staff on duty at the substation. The next day teams arrived from Chelmsford to assist the exhausted rescuers. It was Romford's worst night of the war.

During the Blitz the local Defences did what they could to combat the air attacks. Searchlights at the nearby gun battery at Whalebone Lane raked the sky like laser beams and we could hear the constant thumping of the 'Ack Ack' (Anti-Aircraft) guns. Michael's father, also in the Home Guard, took part on occasions during which time he was shut in and was deaf when he returned home. We have learned that the unmistakeable 'woom woom' misbeat throbbing of the Junkers 88 bombers was because one of their engines rotated fractionally slower than the other and this confused the sound locators on the guns.

Smaller Bofors guns were fired from transporters driven up and down the arterial road at the back of us. Their shells in clips of four were fired in quick succession making a distinctive sound and the guns were named 'pom poms'. Three sizes of HE's (High Explosives) are exhibited at the

Combined Military Services Museum at Maldon in Essex. Their intimidating whistling sound was created by hollow tubes like organ pipes fitted to their fins. The up and down wailing notes of the 'warning' signal of the siren at Collier Row Police Station were joined in quick succession by others en route to the City: Chadwell Heath, Goodmayes, Seven Kings being our nearest. It was a relief eventually to hear the continuous note of the 'All Clear'. Our wardens had to shout 'All Clear' the night ours was silenced by a bomb. Rattles were to be used in the event of a gas attack. My abiding memory is the cacophony of sound: the sirens followed by the Junkers bombers, the 'thump thump' of the 'Ack Ack guns', 'pom pom' of the 'Bofors' and the whistling and exploding bombs. After the 'All Clear' it was uncannily quiet. It was lovely when Springtime arrived to hear the blackbirds singing in the trees as it got light.

Essex Road

'Double Summertime' was introduced on 4th May 1941 to help the war effort in factories and on the land. Later in the year it meant we were going to school in the dark and unfortunately this too caused casualties. Buses had hooded headlamps that didn't project much light and by then people's concentration was impaired by general tiredness and weariness of war. Later in the year lingering fog like a thick enveloping blanket covered everything and impaired vision and hearing. Disorientation could soon overcome pedestrians who had to choke and grope their way about. Our clothing suffered too: white petticoats got streaked and sooty mucous stained our hankies when we blew our noses. Post-War, when Jeanne and I were working in the City, we chose black slips!

If our lights dipped twice during bad raids we knew Dad was busy switching supply and a third dip would probably mean blackout. Strategically placed nightlights, candles and torches were on hand in various places to prevent us colliding with furniture, particularly during the nights when it had been moved. Electricity supplies too had to be cut off when deep craters fractured water mains, ruptured sewers and severed underground cables producing dangerous conditions for buried victims and the rescue crews who needed to dig in the rubble to locate them. The severed cables were 'pot ended' to make them safe but repairs in the blackout were very difficult and sometimes had to wait until daylight. Many barrage balloons were moored in the London area and the cables of drifting ones, brought by prevailing south-westerly winds over Essex, shorted out the overhead lines. The substation staff worked a shift system and were on hand day and night, also fitting in fire watching duties, lessons in first aid and dealing with potential incendiaries as well as Home Guard training. They had camp beds but I don't think they were used much as they were too busy.

The repair crews had a difficult time as they had to carry ladders over their shoulders with their equipment in side carts. They were also called to other districts, as it was imperative to get supply back to hospitals as soon as possible. On 15th October 1940 a bomb at Dagenham had interrupted supply to the Sanatorium there and also Rush Green and Oldchurch Hospitals. With all the juggling of duties Dad got really tired and, when he slept before or after night shifts, Jeanne and I would creep about the house remembering to step over the second step of the stairs which creaked: I wonder if it still does? The substation was close to the arches of Romford railway station at the back of the Havana Cinema and the Brewery was close by. The latter was to be badly damaged on five different occasions throughout the war. Dad related how the staff there, to keep their spirits up, used to put water into an empty whisky barrel, seal it firmly and then kick it around the yard when passing by. When eventually it was opened it produced a 'palatable pick-me-up'!

In December 1940 Aunt Emmie had asked Jeanne and I to be bridesmaids at cousin John Gutteridge's Spring 1941 wedding in Coventry, but its recent bombardment had prompted Mum to decline as she thought we could be going 'out of the frying pan into the fire'. Her fears were to be justified as Jeanne remembers Dad's description of his walk from Euston to Liverpool Street on his return when the City streets were strewn with uncoiled fire hoses and the sky glowing red from the fires still alight. The wedding was towards the end of the week so Dad's return could well have been the night of 10/11th May 1941 described so graphically in Gavin Mortimer's book 'The Longest Night'. It was a moonlit night with no incidents in our immediate area but vast areas of London were devastated. It began soon after midnight when the Thames was at low tide. This and a change in wind direction made the task of the fighters extremely difficult and hazardous.

This raid and earlier ones created a wasteland in the City, but wild flowers managed to thrive. Maybe this inspired Noel Coward's legendary song 'London Pride'. He recorded that it was composed in the Spring of 1941 whilst he was sitting on a damaged London railway station platform and was completed within a few days. Michael and I love the City and have 'handed down our pride` to our son Paul and eldest grandson Craig who are now also 'Freemen of the City`. Like poppies in France during WWI, the 'London Pride' seeds must have drifted from the many bomb sites in the City. A seed from a discarded apple core tossed into a bomb site near St. Pauls was to mature and produce apples before the site was finally to be developed many years later. I remember the devastation in the City when I started working there in 1948. Low brick retaining walls had been built around the gaping holes to prevent people falling into the cavernous basement areas, particularly in fog and at night. One account records there were fifty-seven consecutive nights of bombing on London without respite until May 1941, but local records for Romford show that we had some respite over the Christmas period 1940 and some weekends were also free. Maybe the Germans were repairing their planes for the next onslaught or knew there would be less people in the City? Somehow we managed to cope with it all and the 'bulldog breed' attitude of the British public had refused to give in.

As houses had come down so did class barriers. People from all walks of life rolled up their sleeves, rubbed shoulders and tackled new tasks in the common cause. In November 1939 a new National Savings scheme had been set up and people were urged to save and beat the 'Squander Bug'. Mum volunteered to cover our half of the road and I helped occasionally and soon became better acquainted with neighbours who previously had only exchanged nods. Those with loved ones far away appreciated a brief chat and we soon made friends. The 'Careless Talk Costs Lives' warning wasn't relevant as we all knew each other and preferred to talk about cheerful things. Although rigid class divisions had blended, a few still liked to maintain their dignity and Michael's mother amused us with a story related to her by a friend Mrs. Beamish who lived in Emerson Park the 'posh end' of Hornchurch. In the event of being trapped in a raid she had given her husband strict instructions to remove her curlers before the rescue squad arrived. She would have made a perfect Hyacinth in 'Keeping up appearances'! Stately homes had been taken over for evacuees, safe storage of art treasures from various places and the hospitalisation of wounded servicemen. People from across the class spectrum teamed up in many activities including the visit made by King George VI and Queen Elizabeth to the stricken areas of East London . Michael's cousin Ray Jarvis was one of the escorts of the two Princesses when they were at Windsor. Joyce Grenfell, a niece of the Astors at Cliveden, was a wonderful example for boosting morale wherever she went and is remembered with affection by many.

At Christmas time Mr. Cayford, Dad's colleague, gave him the day shift so that we could enjoy the evening. Jeanne and I took his well-wrapped Christmas lunch to the substation and sat with him whilst he ate it. In the evening the usual family pursuits included the comparatively new board game 'Monopoly'. We didn't put up paper decorations during the Blitz period for safety reasons and, as the War progressed, spare tree bulbs, replacement baubles and tinsel became unobtainable. Rations meant we had limited food for the festive season but Gran always sent us a bird from Somerset and we had a lot of fun.

III

POST-BLITZ ACTIVITIES

In May 1941 Hitler turned his attention to Russia and Luftwaffe bombing attacks on England ceased by the end of July. After the Japanese attack on Pearl Harbour on 7th December the Americans declared War on them the next day and Britain joined with them to protect our interests in the Far East. At last, they then offered assistance to Britain in our war effort; the first American contingent arriving in Northern Ireland on 26th January 1942, in London early in March and others were to be deployed to other parts of England including the West country. This is mentioned later in the run-up to D-Day when they were heavily involved in the final stages of the War. In Essex their fighter and bomber groups occupied around some seventeen airfields in Essex including Weathersfield, Gt. Dunmow, Boxted, Boreham near Chelmsford, Rivenhall and 'Stanstead' (Mountfitchet), which has since become a major airport.

There were bomber stations in various places across England and at Hughendon Manor, code-named 'Hill House', cartographers drew up maps for Bomber Command. The one carried out on the German city of Lubeck on the night of 28th/29th March 1942 was to provoke a similar reaction to the earlier one on Berlin when London was the return target in 1940. The German "Vergeltungsangriffe" retaliatory raids on our cathedral cities in 1942 targeted Exeter, Bath, Norwich and York in April, with Exeter a victim once more in May. Canterbury was to suffer after RAF raids on Cologne at the end of May and beginning of June. In later 'hit-and-run' raids on coastal towns Deal suffered the most with thirty fatalities. Other raids on East Anglia included Bury St. Edmunds, Cambridge, Lowestoft, Gt. Yarmouth and Ipswich where, fortunately, the damage was less severe.

These incidents account for the respite we were having in our area, with only one incident being recorded for 4th September 1942 when an unexploded bomb landed in Rainham. It was during this quieter period that I began dancing classes at the Nimbus Ballroom at the top of Romford Market and I became friendly with Wendy Eavis. Other children attended morning cinema at the Laurie opposite. Known affectionately as the 'flea pit' it gave them entertainment and freedom as well as getting them out from under their busy mums' feet. Michael enjoyed most the Laurel & Hardy escapades. Fleas and head lice had become a nuisance by then and it was on the morning of my Scholarhip exam in March that year that I presented Mum with evidence of an attack on me by the latter. She, who had always kept us 'squeaky clean', was horrified! When I returned from Pettits Lane School the necessary remedies were lined up on the draining board and, after a quick enquiry about the exam, I was head over the sink receiving the first jug of water. My subdued sister had already been dealt with: the culprit being her desk mate. Thank goodness we had bobbed hair! For several days we nit-combed and at school were to be inspected by the 'Nit Nurse', affectionately named by some 'Nitty Norah'.

Laurie Cinema

Cinderella was the panto at this time and I was 'Buttons' with only a few lines to learn, but the song and dance routines took some time to perfect. One day whilst working on Dad's allotment next to the Rex cinema at Collier Row I agreed reluctantly to take part in a talent contest. These were held to boost the takings at matinees. A solo ballet routine on an enormous cinema stage was a challenge and, as I stepped forward to the footlights, the enormity of it all hit me at the same time as the spotlight beam above blinded me as it accompanied me to the microphone at the front of the stage. Feeling like Maria in The Sound of Music at the gates of the Von Trapp chateau I took a deep breath and managed to get through my performance. Not being able to see the audience helped, but I was so relieved when I made my exit. One of the other competitors strode confidently across the stage in bonnet and shawl, swinging a caged stuffed cock linnet and singing "My old man said foller the van..." She was brilliant and came first and years later I was told she was probably Milly Martin, a member of the 'Collier Row Nibs' dancing troupe and later to appear in 'That was the week that was' with David Frost. The experience made me realise that I couldn't make entertainment my career.

I think it was at this time too we were encouraged to take picnics in the countryside to enjoy the fresh air, but Wendy and I had to abandon a trip to Rise Park because of torrential rain. With our picnic set out on a cloth on the floor in the dining room, we watched the pelting rain through the french window. The dancing class performed yearly pantomimes at the Wykeham Hall in the Market Place, giving numerous concerts at other venues for Red Cross funds. Entertainment was limited and I think the general public appreciated our local amateur efforts. For the panto 'Cinderella` that year we bought in the market material not needing clothing coupons for our costumes: white terry towelling for 'I'm dreaming of a white Christmas' and anti-blast window netting for our ballet tutus. The chaos caused by frequent costume changing in the tiny dressing room at Wykeham Hall was dealt with by two unflappable mums who fielded outfits thrown by little ones desperate to be ready on time. 'Shushed` and shuffled by Mums into their correct order, they kept quiet until their cue then pattered on stage looking like little dolls, with rosebud mouths, rouged cheeks and eye shadow. The six 'mice` who pulled Cinderella`s coach onto the stage had to be assisted from the wings by some hefty shoving! Accompanied by a pianist and violinist we sang songs featuring the Armed Forces and cheery ones to keep everyone's spirits up with the audience joining in. At the end everyone stood for the National Anthem and it was a very patriotic time. The little cherubs were then collected by doting mums and taken home way past their bedtime.

I'm including military activities that were in operation at various times which we knew nothing of as it puts things into perspective. During this respite from German attacks we were unaware that on 6th July 1942 a detachment of thirteen Royal Marines had begun training at Southsea for 'Operation Frankton' destined to take place from 7-12th December that year. The Combined Military Services Museum at Maldon in Essex details their heroic endeavours to disrupt German food and raw material supplies which were offloaded at Bordeaux. This involved a canoe journey upriver of around one hundred miles and the placing of limpet mines on their cargo ships anchored there. The mission involving six canoes with two men apiece has been covered in great detail in C.E. Lucas Phillips' *Cockleshell Heroes*. Our food supplies at that time were limited and the weather bitterly cold for standing in queues for non rationed items, but how much colder it must have been paddling silently in icy waters in the dark to complete their mission. One canoe was damaged and its two crew members forced to withdraw. Of the remaining ten taking part two were drowned, six were captured and shot, with the two survivors Captain Hugh Thompson and Marine Clark eventually managing to get back to England at the end of February 1943 after their tortuous journey via an escape route through occupied territories to the coast and eventual freedom. There are two surviving canoes at Maldon Museum; one which failed to take part and the other a sole survivor of the Operation. Winston Churchill said it had helped shorten the war by six months. In the subsequent film depicting their experiences, Trevor Howard starred as the Captain and Anthony Newley as the Marine. Clark's father thought he would never see his son again and their reunion in the film is very moving.

It was in September 1942, two months after their training had begun, that I began five years of studying at Romford County High School for Girls, now called the 'Frances Bardsley', in Upper Brentwood Road. In spite of clothes rationing, which had started in July 1941, full school uniform was obligatory and, as well as the obvious underwear and lisle stockings, we needed house shoes, gym shoes shirt and bloomers, science overalls and art aprons; also panama hats for summer and black velour for winter. This seemed somewhat excessive under the circumstances as many of the girls' fathers were on army pay. When the War started, a private soldier's wage was 2/-d a day and only increased to 3/-d by the end. My uniform took up practically the entire family's clothing coupons by the time we'd acquired everything specified!

Before our first term we attended a 'get together' at the school to meet fellow classmates, familiarize ourselves with the buildings and have short interviews with Miss Chappel the Head Mistress. I eyed with interest the girls who would be with me for the next five years or so and, at my interview, classified Miss Chappel as 'very academic'. When asked my favourite subject I replied with complete honesty "sport" and wondered how I'd be classified. On returning home I was sad to hear that Mr. Macbeth our neighbour had collapsed and died. He was an officer at the Salvation Army Headquarters in Queen Victoria Street and must have been affected by its destruction on the night of 10-11th May 1940 and the subsequent supervision of dealing with the damage and so many people in need. The neighbours had great respect for him and front room curtains were drawn on the day of his funeral. Soon after that our front doorstep dividing fence was removed so that Jeanne or I could fetch Mrs. Mac into our house for company when necessary.

Our school fees for High School were assessed according to our fathers' salaries and, because there were no free bus passes, household budgets were affected. The banning of any jewellery also levelled our status. Before starting our first term we had been sent a book giving basic facts concerning 'reproduction' prior to future biology lessons. Jeanne read it first and then it was my turn. It was a steep learning curve as my mother had been reluctant to enlighten either of us. She was embarrassed when, armed with this new intelligence, I asked Mrs. Mac's newly married daughter Eileen when she was going to have a baby. In due course we were all medically examined and I weighed in at 5st.2lbs. with a height of 4'5". The War by then had taken its toll on transport and the clapped out 247 bus I took to school struggled up Brentwood Road laden with girls and their baggage. We were forbidden to dash to the platform before alighting as the weight would have brought the poor bus to a halt! Knowing the layout of the school helped a lot. As mentioned earlier, I was disappointed they had no library, only a pile of books at the end of the corridor. Maybe the HE dropped in the vicinity during the early hours of 24th October 1940 had been responsible? Books, like so many things, were a precious commodity during the War and our textbooks, printed on recycled paper, were covered with brown wrapping paper and handled with care to prolong their life.

In the first form we soon learned the school rules. Shoulder length hair had to be tied back and one morning at Assembly a miscreant was summoned to the stage for hers to be tied back with string by the Headmistress. In the second year when I was late for a class a teacher called after me "no running in the corridor first former" and I made my escape, relieved that I hadn't been recognised. A few years later, another girl who frequently broke the rules, was to be expelled. We also had deportment training with books balanced on our heads and elocution lessons reminiscent of 'My Fair Lady' when we repeated "The rain in Spain..." and "How now brown cow..." and split into groups to make polite conversation. After practising controlled breathing we stood in turn at the back to read a piece of prose with short breaks for commas and full stops and a three second pause at the end of paragraphs. Before lunch two pupils laid the tables for lunch in the dining room. These were inspected for any incorrect placing of cutlery by a member of staff and mistakes rectified: likewise any girl who held her fork with a 'pencil grip' whilst eating. Fortunately Jeanne and I had been taught at home. Hungry girls who ate chips from a paper bag on the way home were told at Assembly that they were to bring them back to school where plates would be provided. We also had regular nail inspections and it took me some time to kick the habit of biting mine, which had started during the stressful times during the Blitz.

Prior to the Blitz all the school windows had been netted as protection and there were underground and surface shelters. We drilled in procedures for possible raids and had practises: a special ring of the bell, exit by specified doors according to our location and everything to be left on our desks. With about five hundred and fifty girls and thirty staff speed was essential and we were allowed to run through the corridors! I believe we came first in a competition amongst local schools. There were various activities during lunch breaks and after school. I wouldn't join the rabbit club as I couldn't bear the thought that they would end up in someone's cooking pot. As winter approached we were given navy blue wool to knit socks for sailors, but when raids resumed I had little time after dancing classes coupled with homework and turning heels with four needles in bad light was difficult!

My start at High School in 1942 had coincided with Hitler's offensive in Russia and eventual endeavours to take the Russian city of Stalingrad. Heavy bombing and shelling and subsequent efforts to starve them into submission failed. His own troops with inadequate clothing, food, fuel and ammunition supplies suffered equally. Eventually in the sub zero temperatures many of them, including newly recruited teenagers, froze to death. In spite of Hitler's refusal to allow them to surrender, all the German Commanders-in-Chief capitulated: one group on 31st January 1943 and the other on February 2nd. Civilians had suffered too, particularly the elderly and mothers with young children. It was also very cold in England and Jeanne suffered badly with chilblains and I remember a shopping trip when mum took me into Marks & Spencer for a hot drink when my hands froze and my head began to spin. It must have been so much worse in Russia.

Ordinary day-to-day life continued for all of us with Michael travelling daily to school by steam train from Romford. The engine crews had experienced difficult times during the Blitz in the winter of 1940 and I've learned since that they endeavoured to get their engines into a tunnel or under a bridge at night to conceal the firebox glow. During daylight they had stopped, because the steam and movement would have made them easy targets. Michael started at Mercers School in Holborn in September 1942 and did some of his homework whilst travelling home from Liverpool Street. On the morning of 12th March 1943 a low flying German plane, making an escape dash to the east coast via the railway line, fired its machine guns en route forcing passengers awaiting their train at Romford to dive for cover. Michael's train was delayed and, as it proceeded slowly from the station, he said the top of a gasometer, which had been peppered with bullets, looked like an enormous gas ring. Two brave fire fighters wearing asbestos suits climbed up to plug the holes. The Brewery nearby was also caught by incendiaries and Dad mentioned the incident when he returned home from his shift at the substation sited beneath the station.

Repairing the gasometer

The RAF were doing all they could during this time and in June 1943 a 'Wings for Victory Week' was launched with each town setting targets for the purchase of replacement aircraft. Hornchurch raised £348,505 and Romford £341,000; incredible amounts at that time. At High School we had a poster competition and I traced outlines of the fighters from newspaper pictures and added an appropriate slogan. Apparently, Spitfires were already in production in 1937, and in 1939, just prior to our evacuation to Somerset, deliveries were being made to RAF squadrons.

Fortunately we had few incidents from the air after that, but by the beginning of 1943, information from European sources was being sent to Allied Intelligence of the development of Hitler's latest weapons the VI: the VII rocket was to come later. The general public didn't know this and also that Airborne Paratroopers were to begin their training in May for their vital role at the forefront of the D-Day landings in Normandy in June 1944. In September 1943 in my second year at High School I began the battle of learning Latin which I found a challenge and would have preferred German instead. Fraulein Kalmein the teacher was well respected and no-one queried her origins. Internees had been released in

1942 so maybe she was a German or Austrian Jew who'd come to England for safety? The Mercers School, which Michael and his brother Peter attended, didn't teach German until the end of the War. I found lessons and homework demanding and, like a lot of people, was weary with the strain of coping with things generally.

I had got on well with most of the girls but had never been invited to join a group. A close relationship hadn't materialised as I tended to observe rather than plunge into anything more to avoid disappointment on either side if it didn't work. By this time I was taking sandwiches for lunch and teamed up with Phyllis Smith: she must have forgotten that I'd tied her long plaits together over the bar of her chair in front of me in the first form! Although outwardly reserved I discovered she had a great sense of humour and we enjoyed our companionship. By this time too we had new neighbours when Mr & Mrs. Bolton, Trevor and Doreen, moved in next door from Ilford. House prices were at rock bottom as no-one wanted to commit themselves during wartime.

The donkey outside M & S

Before Christmas 1943 Trevor and I went to Romford to look for family presents. Although the market stalls ranged along the cobbles were welcoming with the glow from their hissing Tilley lamps and cheery banter of the stallholders, items were restricted and the main shops in the

High Street were drab and cheerless with their boarded up windows. It was a bitterly cold day and, along with several others, we stopped outside Marks & Spencers where a donkey was collecting money for cigarettes for the troops. The donkey didn't look too happy and as I stepped forward to stroke it a flash photo was taken. A few years ago we discovered the picture in Brian Evans` book *Romford, Collier Row & Gidea Park*: Trevor peering over my shoulder and Michael at the end of top row left. [At that time Michael was "the polite boy up the road who touched his cap when we passed."]

Romford's last bombing raid was in the early hours of 19th April 1944 when many standard and explosive incendiaries were dropped over a wide area with the Brewery a victim once more. The Combined Military Services Museum at Maldon have a 'scatterbomb' carrier. About 5'9" in height, it could carry 133 standard incendiary bombs and when released it split open distributing them over a wide area creating huge fires. Exploding ones had been introduced as a deterrent to fire fighters and were classified as 'I.B.W.S.E.N' [Incendiary Bombs with Separating Exploding Nose]. The first to land in our vicinity landed in Pettits Lane, the next on Mr. Newton's bungalow about 100 yds. from us and another one really close in the rear garden of Mr. Butterworth's bungalow on Eastern Avenue. Having escorted his wife to the shelter first, he sustained injuries to the back of his legs on his return trip for their dog. His dividing fence was soon ablaze and threatening to spread to our section two doors away. Dad tackled the fire with a small gauge garden hose and was soaked when the full pressure of a Fire Service hose threw him backwards We were so worried about his safety and all laughed with relief when he returned safely to the shelter thoroughly soaked!

Wooden Class Rooms

Havering Road 'Parklands' school was to be the next target in line from us and received a considerable number of incendiaries. The wooden block

of classrooms by the playing fields was a near miss when sever'
very close to it. A direct hit would have reduced it to ashes i'
The casualties in the area generally were five, also one f.
damage to twenty-eight houses. Mr Newton, a fire fighter on duty ⌐
time, was dealing with fires in another area, but fortunately his wife and
twin daughters were OK on his return.

By then I was at Romford County High School, but details of the
incident in the diary of Havering Road School give graphic details of the
event and the eventual reopening of the premises. The following precis
from three full pages, gives details of the event and eventual re-opening
of the school. The casualties in the area generally were five, also one
fatality and damage to twenty-eight houses.

'April 19 - Duty firewatchers, the Headmaster and two female staff
extinguished one in the Ladies Lavatory passage and a fire in Infants
classroom 9. Two reinforcement stirrup pump parties dealt with two
exploding ones which landed on the Hall, penetrating the platform and
igniting forms stored beneath, but their efforts combined with those of
the N.F.S. (National Fire Service) failed to prevent the complete
gutting of the Hall ...

The Headmaster's thanks to all for their splendid assistance whilst
subjected to acrid fumes and smoke is followed by a complete
inventory of all the items destroyed.

'April 19- School closed due to unexploded bombs on premises.'

'April 24 - School re-opened. During week-end ARP 'Air Raid
Precaution` personnel removed 52 unexploded bombs from school
grounds. 14 dining tables and 30 forms received from Dagenham.

Michael and I are extremely grateful to the school's Office Manager Viv
Mangan for arranging our visit in 2009 and Pete Johnson their IT
Manager who escorted us around. We were aware of the happy
atmosphere and particularly enjoyed the childrens' mural display of Walt
Disney characters lining the corridors as we both remember the release of
his film 'Snow White & the Seven Dwarfs' in 1938.

IV

THREE R'S: RATIONING, RECYCLING, RENOVATION

Whilst coping with raids and restrictions generally we were also mastering the three R's: Rationing, Recycling and Renovation.

1. RATIONING: The rigours of rationing began on January 8th 1940. Constant attacks on our merchant shipping by the German navy during the first ten months of the war caused the loss of 2,300,000 tons of precious food supplies and this was to continue. Older people had experienced rationing during WWI, but it was to be a new discipline for the next generation, who had to accept the fact that food would be limited and children had to learn they would no longer be able to spend their pocket money on sweets or snacks when they felt like it. Each family was registered and our ration books were issued from Romford's Food Office at the corner of Pettits Lane and Main Road. The adult book was buff, blue for 8-15 years and green for nursing and expectant mums and babies, with priorities being given accordingly. We had to stay with our chosen outlets until the next issue of books as supplies allocated to retailers tallied with their number of registered customers.

Mr. Morris in Victoria Road provided our groceries. The adult rations per week were: butter 2oz, margarine 4oz, cooking fat 2-4oz and cheese 2 oz or 8-16 for people doing heavy work. Bacon and ham were 4 oz. Bought preserves were 1 lb. per person every two months and I think 4 oz. of marmalade. The 8 oz. of sugar included cooking requirements and was increased during the jam making and fruit bottling season. The WI, the 'Jam & Jerusalem Brigade' contributed to the supply of the latter products. Novice housewives found it a 'testing time' when turning bottled fruit jars upside down to check their seals. Sales of bottling equipment must have rocketed and the corks of home-brewing attempts frequently did!

The weekly tea ration of 2 oz. per person was eked out as much as possible, being kept for use during raids and times of stress. Fresh shell eggs were in very short supply, varying from one each per week and sometimes longer. They were to be on ration until 1953. Country folk and those who kept chickens in their gardens were more fortunate. Mr. Morris assured my mother that two odorous eggs she took back in a lidded jar must be all right, but when she removed the lid he retreated hurriedly to the rear of the shop! Their developing embryos meant a broody hen had probably been responsible. The dried egg allowance of one packet each per month contained the rough equivalent of one dozen eggs. Like tinned milk, it was used mainly for cooking and produced reasonable results.

Mr Copsey also in Victoria Road supplied our meat, the weekly allowance per person being 1/2d. or 6p in today's metric. This gave us about three meat meals with the Sunday joint taking the most and humbler cuts for the rest. Dripping saved from the joint provided a tasty snack on toast with a scrape of marmite. One week the joint was so tough that Mum enquired the source of the 'mountain goat'! She had to do the best with what she was given and I considered her protests to be justifiable. Leftovers were put through a mincer to make them more edible and were accompanied by a hash of 'bubble and squeak' from left over vegetables. Well-mashed potatoes were added to pastry to increase the topping for pies. Sausages contained less than 10% meat and weren't rationed so it was a question of luck and the goodwill of the butcher. Although not rationed initially, offal was at times part of the allowance.

According to availability adults had two maybe three pints of liquid milk per week and children three and a half. Its distribution was to be controlled from November 1941. We had an additional third of a pint daily at school, Michael often having two and a half pints when several of his friends declined theirs. In December 1941 dried milk arrived: full cream 'National Dried' for young babies and skimmed 'Household' for others, each family being allowed a tin a month. Yielding about four pints when whisked in water it was used mostly for cooking, as it was insipid in tea.

We missed our pre-war cornets and iced lollies when the Walls' "Stop Me and Buy One" ice cream tricycles disappeared from the streets. They were to reappear temporarily in late 1944.

From December points were issued for items in short supply giving shoppers choice of purchases: sixteen per person per month initially, raised for a while and then reduced. Sixteen for a tin of meat or fish or 2 lb. of dried fruit or preserves. 'Sham' raspberry jam was processed from parsnip with appropriate colouring and miniscule wood chippings for pips. We each had 12 oz. of sweets a month and, to make them last, we cut our Mars bars into thin slices. After saving his quota for about six months Michael would share them with his family. Our teeth were probably in better condition and the sparse diet meant we were healthier than today's overweight people. We find we still can't tackle enormous meals. Although Jeanne and I weren't 'picky' we had difficulty in eating tapioca because of its 'frog spawn' consistency. Mum could only get what was available but managed to obtain some semolina to mix with the next offering. We eyed it with suspicion and on enquiring about its contents were told it was 'mystery pudding.'

Tinned fish and meat were useful particularly when military operations in the Pacific began in 1941 causing a reduction in fresh food supplies from Australia and New Zealand which were needed by American troops. Under the US Lend-Lease Agreement we received tins of corned beef and Spam [Supply Pressed American Meat]: a small tin 17 points and the large 54. Eventually it was to become a statutory portion of our meat ration and was dished up in many ways. The 'Lend-Lease` credit with the States was to cease in 1945 when the Japanese surrendered. The interest that had been accrued wasn't, I believe, to be settled finally until the end of 2006.

Michael has always liked cooking and was disappointed when his offers to help during the War were declined because of shortages and his possible failures. My mother, a great fan of Marguerite Patten, liked making her egg less boiled fruit cake whenever possible and visitors enjoyed it. Small amounts of tea, sugar and fat were taken when we visited friends to save depleting their supplies. Crockery was handled with great care as breakages were catastrophic and replacements virtually unobtainable by 1941. Cracked and chipped items weren't always discarded and some practical people used enamelware as it 'bounced.' Our everyday set of Hitchman's Dairy ware managed to survive pretty well and the complete china dinner and tea service was kept 'for best` and only came out for Christmas. In this way we just managed to last for the duration. I realise how lucky we were compared with some families who were forced to use empty jam jars for drinking vessels. I remember after the War going with my mother by bus to Moultons Store in Ilford to bring back a full new set of everything in white 'Utility' china and then staggering back with them trying not to drop anything!

Land countrywide had been acquired compulsorily to produce the maximum amount of food. Cousin Geoffrey Prole, who had been taken from Kent to his aunt's home in Wheddon Cross on Exmoor in Somerset, has told us that bowler hatted men with brief cases came from the Ministry to their area to assign suitable land for ploughing. Despite advice from the local farmer that his land was unsuitable due to flooding, the planting of potatoes and sewing of wheat went ahead and the eventual crops soon blackened and the quality was poor. Other areas of countryside were utilised also including the South Downs. Large parks were cultivated and land drainage pipes used where necessary. It was to take quite a long time for everything to return to Nature after the War.

The (WLA) Women's Land Army made tremendous efforts to supply us with food and we owe them a lot. Their pay was 10/-d. a week or 50 pence in metric and this had to cover all their needs including replacement uniform. There were around 80,000 of them and their hours varied according to the time of year: Double Summertime meant they worked long hours until dusk. Sugar beet was grown extensively which was a great help when cane sugar supplies from the West Indies were being hampered. The tremendous increase in wheat production meant that flour wasn't rationed, but later it was to be necessary to ration bread and potatoes.

The threat to shipping meant that bananas and oranges were only available for infants so Jeanne and I had to go without for the duration of the War. Locally produced fruit and vegetables were not rationed and consequently queues were very long. The housewives' tenacity was acknowledged by Winston Churchill with a quote from a poem by John Milton, 'They also serve who only stand and wait.' I accompanied my mother when possible and stood in another queue hoping to get things she missed. Sometimes there were so many people that the lines were split into two to aid the passage of pedestrians. Opportunists who tried

I make a good Soup!

Says 'POTATO PETE'

DOCTOR CARROT
the
Children's
best
friend

joining the end of the first half were quickly put right! Folk watched anxiously as the fruit and veg. diminished as it was so disappointing to reach the stall to be told "that's it" as the stallholder turned his scoop upside down and we had to join another line. There were no paper bags either and things were just tipped into our shopping bags. I remember the occasion when an assistant was well through Mum's order when the boss told her she couldn't have them as she wasn`t a regular customer. After this second lengthy wait she was so upset and frustrated that she tipped the basket upside down, leaving him to collect the scattered produce whilst we searched once more. Knitted or crocheted bags wore well and were more of a deterrent to pilfering. On another occasion Mum came home very upset, as someone had 'lifted' some of her purchases from the top of her basket.

Whilst the next door house remained vacant we were allowed to pick the annual crop of Bramley and eating apples and climbing the trees was much more fun than waiting for ages in a long queue without getting any. Blackberries were picked from bushes in Rise Park and we were encouraged to gather rose hips for syrup as they were rich in vitamin C. Urged to 'Dig for Victory', allotments had sprung up on every conceivable piece of spare ground which even included some railway embankments where safe. Our garden was cleared except for the roses between which we grew tomato plants, with salad and veg. being grown in the other borders. The dug up car park of the Rex Cinema at Collier Row provided another plot to which Dad and I cycled regularly with tools strapped to his cross bar. The National Trust also had given access to some of their suitable areas. Today the desire for fresh organic vegetables has created a demand for plots and initially there were 100,000 people on waiting lists.

Because fresh fish wasn't rationed there were always long queues in Romford at Thompsons in North Street and MacFisheries in South Street.

Fried fish and chips were in great demand from Sudders in North Street and spare newspapers welcomed. During long spells of waiting I'd beat the boredom by watching their techniques of production. They worked tirelessly: washing potatoes, pounding them through the chipper whilst fish fillets were flapped through flour, stroked through batter and lowered rhythmically into the sizzling fat. This could easily have been set to music and reminds me now of the masterful 'Morecombe & Wise' breakfast routine! We hoped the supplies wouldn't run out, but some unfortunate people had to return home without. Fast food outlets today mean that 'couch potatoes`, via modern technology, can text for home delivery of various meals without even getting up!

The British Restaurant at the Good Shepherd church hall at Collier Row provided us with a good meal on a day when our cupboard was extra bare. We had boiled bacon, pease pudding and mashed potato followed by 'spotted dick' with custard and a cup of tea. Reasonably priced at just over l/-d. or 7p. in metric they were good value and essential for people who had no cooking facilities because of recent bombing. Mobile Canteens manned by the WVS also provided sustenance for Civil Defence Volunteers and victims of recent bombing who had no cooking facilities of their own. Founded in 1938, they were to provide many services throughout the war including the evacuation of young evacuees forced to leave their homes for various reasons and in particular the troops returning from Dunkirk.

Each Christmas Gran sent a bird of some sort from Somerset, which was gratefully received. On one occasion postal delays meant a late arrival and my mother, like Dickens' Mrs. Cratchit in *Christmas Carol* wondered what we'd have. When it finally arrived it was a goose fully clothed! My mother being country born and bred was used to plucking, disembowelling, singeing and dressing birds, but progress faltered at the early stage when it refused to part company with its wing feathers! Undaunted we went out to the garage where she sat with it clutched on her lap whilst I removed them one by one with a stout pair of pliers, catapulting backwards as each one yielded. It amused us a lot and we also enjoyed the bird, which lasted for days, and I still have the enormous plate on which it was kept warm in front of the fire.

In spite of rationing and other limitations we enjoyed Christmas and relatives who lived near enough would try to get together. The following are recollections of those days written by Michael and entitled 'A Christmas Poem':

When I was young a kind of magic shone through Christmas Day,
For we had special food to eat and simple games to play.
We'd have a hand-made toy or two an apple and some sweets,

and if the rations stretched that far some other little treats.
We'd have a chicken Christmas lunch and then the King we'd hear
speaking on the wireless and wishing us good cheer.
Then we would choose some records on the gramophone to play,
something which we only did upon a special day,
And grandparents and uncles and aunts and cousins too
would all join in and play the games, that's what we used to do.
But now the table groans with food, the drinks come thick and fast
The children have so many gifts and none of them will last.
They play with their computer games which no one can join in,
so all the family joys have gone it really is a sin.
And when I'm home when all is done and sitting in my chair,
the ghosts of all those now passed on come visiting me there.
And happy dreams I have of them the joy and all the mirth,
and then I have to thank my God for Jesus Christ on earth.

We are fortunate as our grandchildren when young enjoyed family games and now we all enjoy TV or have conversations on topics of interest.

The strict rationing made us very careful with food and we never wasted anything. By habit I still scrape butter and margarine wrappers and remove the last remnants from containers. Fifteen thousand Dutch people were to die of starvation in the winter of 1944/5 and, before hostilities ceased, the Germans arranged a cease-fire so that our planes could drop relief supplies. Today's 'sell by' dates prompt the unnecessary throwing away of an enormous amount of food because people don't check in time. A BBC2 TV programme some time ago revealed that £500 worth of food per family was being tipped annually into landfill sites. An update on this [2016] was a comment by Stephen Cottrell, Bishop of Chelmsford that "UK homes waste an estimated 7 million tonnes of food and drink each year." I reflect sadly on the millions of people around the world who are starving, particularly when we see almost full polystyrene chip containers discarded in the streets or alongside the verges of roads. Meat continued to be rationed until 1954 when rationing finally was to end. We had often been hungry but could do nothing about it, but restrictions then and the improved medical facilities of today probably account for the increase in the elderly population as we still can't tackle large meals.

Increased demand for coal for the war effort meant that household supplies had to be rationed. Too many miners having been conscripted into the Forces it became necessary by mid-1943 to seek volunteers. Few came forward as other jobs were more inviting. In December with the weather deteriorating and only about three weeks' supply remaining,

Coalition Labour MP Ernest Bevin, Minister of Labour & National Service, appealed for volunteers and then a random lottery scheme was set up. If the last number of the recruit's National Service registration number coincided with the number drawn he became a miner. It was really tough for those who had been hoping to enlist in the Forces, but it was a time when everyone had to adapt.

Their name 'Bevin Boys' derived from Ernest Bevin's speech when he announced that 72,000 were needed continuously to be employed in the industry and that "This is where you boys come in." We owe a great deal to all the miners who made such an effort to 'Keep the Home Fires Burning' and maintain energy supplies for the factories. It wasn't easy for the new recruits and a post-War work colleague of Michael recalled how he hadn't enjoyed a roof fall after which he and his friends had to wait for a break-through for their release. We had registered for our ration at an office near Romford station and by January 1944 were restricted to four cwt. per month. It was like gold dust and my mother counted each precious sack hoisted off the lorry and carried through to the coal shed. I don't think we bothered with the unrationed 'Nutty Slack' as its quality was poor. It was to be used for the manufacture of breeze blocks in post-war rebuilding. Getting a fire going was difficult at times and sheets of newspaper held across the front would 'boof' up the chimney when it ignited. In winter we'd huddle round it adding lumps sparingly to keep it going and I enjoyed lying on the floor to watch particles of soot igniting and chasing each other up the chimney creating moving pictures.

Coal Delivery Lorry

The back boiler provided hot water when we did take a bath, but often needed supplementing with water heated in the Burco wash boiler and carried in buckets up to the bathroom. The statutory amount allowed was five inches and it was a chilly experience as we splashed it over us as it cooled. We used a paraffin heater as the small electric fire was banned from the bathroom for safety reasons: from an early age we had been taught that "electricity and water don't mix." Baths had been abandoned during the Blitz because of the risk of being trapped unclothed, particularly in the winter. We coined the phase that we "washed up as far as possible and down as far as possible"! On really cold mornings when the inside of the windows were encrusted with thick frost I'd crawl to the end of the bed, blow and scrape a hole to see how severe it was outside and then take my underclothes into bed to warm them before dressing. My hot water bottle yielded tepid water for a quick wash before breakfast.

2. RECYCLING: Salvage had been introduced in 1940 and the chain link fencing from our front gardens collected along with pots, pans, mugs and other items. We now know that a lot of it was left to rust and recent excavations in Germany have revealed a quantity which was dropped there by the RAF during the War. The removal of kitchenware was to be unfortunate for people whose remaining utensils wore out as replacements were virtually unobtainable. Pig swill bins at regular intervals along the road collected our kitchen waste: thankfully ours was on the opposite pavement as in hot weather it was a mecca for flies. It was meant to be taken away regularly for boiling but I'm sure a lot must have been useless. The remnants of one of our Sunday joints had to be discarded after a blow fly managed to get into our larder. Biology lessons had given me graphic details of their habits and the family had to duck as I whizzed around the house with a rolled up newspaper shouting "you don't know where it's been!"

Michael's reaction was much more controlled and his mother recalled how he covered carefully all exposed food. Recently, BBC II TV revealed that the pig population in England has declined by 60% since WWII.

The entry of the Japanese into the war in December 1941 and their occupation of palm oil producing areas in East Asia caused a severe shortage of soap. We squeezed together small pieces for hand washing and fragments were put in a metal whisk for washing-up. Newspapers were torn into squares and hung on a piece of string to be used as toilet paper and I remember the old telephone directory torn off page-by-page which we pressed into service. They certainly didn't pass a comfort test and we would wait anxiously to see if they blocked the waste pipe! All available waste paper was salvaged, pulped and used again for books etc. but the quality wasn't very good and writing paper was very thin. Batteries for torches too were virtually unobtainable and candles were used sparingly. Paper clips and drawing pins were saved in tins and we hoarded rubber bands: I'm still tempted to pick up ones discarded by postmen! In 1943 we were urged to 'Make-do & Mend'. Worn sheets were cut in half lengthways with the outside edges flat seamed at the centre and the raw edges made good at the sides. Pillowcases were made from oddments and dusters from worn out flannelette sheets. Dresses were given false hems or were handed down to siblings. Collars on shirts were turned and, if they were too worn out, the tails were cut off to make replacements. Our neighbour remembers having a yellow tail replacement as this was the only material available and he had to keep pushing it down to hide it!

3. RENOVATION. Neighbours brought electrical appliances, watches and clocks for Dad to repair. Mums with husbands away in the Forces were grateful when he repaired irons as these were virtually unobtainable and faulty ones lethal if used. I soon learned the correct procedure for wiring and plug connections. He kept his tools and equipment in the garage along with neatly labelled tobacco tins and glass jars with lids fixed under the shelves with contents easily visible. He used a magnifying glass attachment to his glasses for watches and I marvelled at how he managed to get all the tiny pieces back in the right place. He willingly took on the repairs, bless him, but it meant he didn't get much spare time for relaxation when off duty.

The patchwork of replaced tiles on damaged roofs indicated the areas most affected by enemy action. Panes of glass for repairing windows were in demand and, having cut them out, Dad taught me how to putty them in. Peeled paintwork had to be touched up with remnants of paint mixed together which produced a khaki finish. Final dregs of colours dribbled on upended jam jars made them attractive as well as useful. Interior walls were freshened up with a couple of coats of whitewash and stippled in a different colour with a small sponge to add interest. Spells in the kitchen with Mum and in the garage at Dad's elbow during the six years of War taught me many skills and I soon became expert in housewifery, decorating and repairs and my era of 'DIY' took off.

Meanwhile, back in 1943 as stocks of everything in the shops began to run out, signs were hung up saying "Sorry no more... today" and a rash of chalked cheeky 'Chads' appeared on hoardings etc. announcing the lack of specific items. Clinging onto a wall with fingers and long beaky nose with a wisp of hair question mark on his bald head, the inscription beneath "WOT NO" declared the item in short supply. It was graffiti, but a touch of humour appreciated by Brits. in difficult times. Our friend Ronald Bond whose father had a shop in Ilford remembers the umpteenth customer coming in for cigarettes when a notice outside stated there were none. The exasperated young Ron, whom I might say is very polite, was rebuked soundly by his father when he had replied "Can't you read?"

Few toys or games were available for birthday or Christmas presents. Using a pack of 'Snow White & The Seven Dwarfs' playing cards I drew templates for cut-out wooden models for Mrs. Mac's son-in-law Eric. He produced them and I painted them in their appropriate colours with their names on black slotted bases. They made a good early learning recognition toy for Eric's young son. Another neighbour Miss Kerr who worked for a woman's magazine, gave me felt pieces for four prototype soft toy animals for a future publication. All these, plus homework and a Jemima Puddleduck in Craftwork at school, kept me busy, but it was therapeutic and satisfying to be creating something during the uncertain times in which we were living.

V

COMPARATIVE CALM BEFORE THE STORM

We had a reasonably quiet time in our immediate area through 1942/43 with only intermittent Luftwaffe attacks, which included the machine-gunning incident on the railway in March 1943, but incidents were to increase in 1944.

The German forces in Russia had already suffered badly in the winter of 1941/2 when their supplies of food, fuel and armaments were eventually to peter out due to the appalling weather conditions when sub zero temperatures halted their supplies by road and grounded their planes. Their ill clad troops including underage recruits were half starved and dying. The young ones could only have been five or six years older than me and must have suffered so much and I couldn't have wished that on anyone. Eventually the battle for Stalingrad was to be the end for the Germans who, apart from a small isolated group, surrendered on 31st January 1943.

Uncle Ern from Timberscombe recounted some experiences he had whilst his ship was on escort duty with the British convoys engaged in operation "Archangel", the transportation of tanks and weapons to the Soviet Union for the offensive on the Eastern Front. He said the rough seas hadn't bothered him and most of the injuries sustained were from shifting tanks. Fortunes fluctuated on both sides for the German and Russian Forces throughout the Eastern offensive, including the prolonged Siege of Leningrad, which cost the lives of over more than a million civilians who refused to give in. During this conflict with the Germans, Stalin had been pressing for the opening of the Second Front.

In the Spring of 1943 information was received from Polish sources of the Germans' experimentation with jet propelled rockets: more later. In May 1943, after concentrated training of crews, that the famous 'Dambusters' raid took place on the Mohne and Eder dams, which supplied hydroelectric power to the industrial area of the Ruhr Valley. Practise sorties by Lancaster bombers had been carried out over suitable reservoirs across England including Abberton near Colchester; the first test with Barnes Wallis' bomb being at the Elan Valley in Wales. At the Derwent Reservoir in Derbyshire in October 1986 a commemorative flight was to be made by a lone surviving Lancaster bomber from RAF

Coningsby.

In November 1943 in spite of a slight heart attack, Winston Churchill went to Canada to make plans for the D-DAY landings and their troops began training. Our 6th Airborne Division was formed and also began training and they were all to be the spearhead of the Invasion of Europe in June 1944.

Lancaster 'Dambusters'

Leading up to Christmas Wendy and I had been rehearsing the next panto with Wendy as "Red Riding Hood" and I her "Prince Charming" (see our photograph on the opposite page). Rehearsals had to be juggled with increased homework, which left little time for anything else. Our costumes didn't take much material and some could be worn afterwards. Clothes rationing which had begun at Whitsun 1941 meant we had to make our clothes last as long as possible and by the end of 1943 those who hadn't a good supply when the War began were feeling shabby.

Shops were looking shabby too, many of them with boarded up windows and with little stock. On one shopping trip with Mum my hands were freezing and when my head began to spin she took me into Marks & Spencer for a hot drink. Just before Christmas next door neighbour Trevor and I visited Romford market for last minute presents. It looked festive and the warmth from the hissing Tilley lamps hanging from the stalls ranged along the cobbles and the cheery banter of the market traders helped to create a Christmas atmosphere, which warded off the bitterly cold weather.

Wendy and I in 'panto' costume

Plans for the Invasion of Europe were kept very secret and during the spring of 1944 areas within ten miles of the coast from the Wash to Land's end were out of bounds to visitors whilst preparations were made. Dad and I used to cycle along the Arterial road towards Southend for exercise and would turn back at the "no go" point. People there were turned out of their houses for the billeting of British troops prior to the Invasion. We know someone who was bombed out in London, moved to a flat in

Southend and then into a house to settle permanently, only to be turned out once more. The marshalling of equipment too was a major operation. Mulberry harbours were included and at low tide the remains of one which foundered can, I think, still be seen at low tide on a sandbank.

Wykeham Hall

It was in April '44 the Allies began intensive bombing of areas to be involved in the impending invasion of northern France which included coastal defences, railways, bridges, communications, radar and also V weapon sites being prepared near Calais. These missions were to cost the lives of many airmen and their aircraft. We had no idea when an invasion would take place but just before the event Uncle Cecil Prole who was garrisoned at Colchester visited us at Romford. On another day Uncle Ern Ray turned up from Tilbury where his medical ship was moored prior to sailing. Their short passes meant they couldn't get down to Somerset. I remember going to the Post Office with Uncle Ern where he posted a short letter to Aunty Kath, bashfully putting S.W.A.L.K, 'Sealed with a loving kiss' across the flap. He was to have some terrible memories of the aftermath of the Normandy landings.

In the west country various beaches comparable with those in Normandy had been used to train the Allied troops: the British at Braunton Sands and Woolacombe in north Devon and the Americans on the coast in the Start Bay area of south Devon. The latter had been taken over in November 1943 and occupied by December. The farming folk had to abandon their homes, leave crops in the ground and received low prices for livestock sold. Apparently the milking cows, which they took with them when they were evacuated, made their way to their allotted stalls in the parlours on their eventual return. Wild life and birds also returned to their habitat in the scarred landscape. We have spent countless holidays at Torcross with Howard Garner at Greyhomes. American officers were billeted there whilst preparations and training were in progress prior to the D-Day landings. The surface scars in the dining room panelling from their darts are now barely noticeable. On a visit to the Nature Reserve we were shown trees scarred by the shelling and where live shells had been hidden under the road bridge into Slapton by GI's who'd not wanted to fire them at their buddies during training.

Start Bay, South Devon

When we look out over the beautiful view of Start Bay we remember the tragic loss of lives during exercise Tiger on 28th April 1944, more being killed than in the D-Day landings. The event is covered extensively in Ken Small's book *The Forgotten Dead*. Hospitals throughout the south west dealt with the injured and on their recovery they were sent to various camp sites to prepare for D-Day. Many of those who died were buried secretly somewhere in the South Hams. A re-wording of a sonnet, written by Rupert Brooke during WWI, could sum up their final sacrifice: 'there's some corner in a Devon field that is forever America'. The survivors were to take part in the Invasion, which began on 6th June 1944, four years after the evacuation from Dunkirk. This time the ships were to be taking the war to the Germans and eventual victory.

A neighbour of ours in Little Baddow, Leslie McMillan had also been in South Devon preparing for the Invasion and was involved in exercise "Tiger". A keen yachtsman he had sailed to the French coast to collect samples from the beaches for the planners to ascertain the most suitable landing areas. As "Commander Landing Barges Western Task Force" he sailed with a convoy of ninety-four ships to land equipment and supplies under fire for the Americans on the Omahah and Utah beaches. Media coverage of this has since given graphic details of the experiences of all those involved. He was to be awarded the Legion of Merit, Degree of Commander, with a citation by President Roosevelt: the highest honour given to a non-American for his involvement prior to the landings.

Points of departure for the invading Allied Forces were from Felixstowe in the east to Falmouth in the south-west and also Cardiff and Swansea. The marshalling of all the fighting forces plus all the ancillary services must have been a gigantic planning operation. Mulberry Harbours were amongst the first equipment to arrive, being towed over and placed in position ready for the arrival of the main Forces. The rendezvous area, centred from the Isle Wight to the Baie de Seine on the Normandy coast, was named Piccadilly Circus. Having been delayed by the weather the first sailing took place in the early hours of 6th June 1944 and when they reached Normandy the Americans, British and Canadians landed on their designated beaches: from East to West they were named Utah and Omaha for the Americans and Gold, Juno and Sword for the British and Canadians.

A few years before he died in a nursing home at Minehead in the 1990's Uncle Ern Ray told us of his experiences including the Normandy Landings. He was on the hospital ship Duke of Rothesay, a converted Irish ferryboat, leaving Tilbury in Essex at 3 a.m. on D-Day. With rudders at both ends it was easy to manoeuvre, could make the same speed each way and was ideal for shallow waters. He told us he was below deck when they left and when he went up on deck at daylight at around 4.30am they were surrounded on all sides to the horizon by a mass of ships in every direction as far as the eye could see. His ship was under the command of the American 1st Army General Patton whose troops were to make the Omahah and Utah landings and the Rothesay was to be the first hospital ship to get back with casualties.

The ship had an operating theatre, fifty-four medical corps personnel, one hundred and twenty crew members and could deal with two hundred walking casualties and seven hundred bedridden. Uncle Ern spent the whole time giving morphine injections every four hours, applying tourniquets and making up beds. No matter how badly injured a Canadian might have been they couldn't be put in a bed adjacent to a wounded German. One account of the extended battle for Caen recording the savage assassination by SS Panzer troops of wounded Canadians on the ground and subsequent rounding up POW's may explain their behaviour?

Duke of Rothesay

The Duke of Rothesay was to make sixty-two trips across the Channel after the landings and subsequent fighting. Uncle mentioned an occasion when a unidentifiable body retrieved from the sea had to be incinerated in the ship's boiler. He was drenched by the water released from it when it was lifted and had to take a thorough shower. He was visibly upset as he talked about the terrible injuries with which they dealt. With his head in his hands he was trying to drain away his memories but they kept flooding back. A young eighteen-year-old lad who had been training to be a jockey had lost both his arms and legs. Another was a cook with a damaged spleen who was from a minesweeper, which had been involved in clearing the Channel. As the Rothesay approached Dover he asked to see the White Cliffs and, having seen them through the porthole, died in uncle's arms after being settled back. In their short breaks the orderlies had been told to go below to try to forget about things, but Uncle told us he would never forget and I'm sure it affected him permanently.

David Capps, the husband of Michael's cousin Dorothy, sailed on D-Day+1 the 7th June 1944 and was involved in the fighting for Caen which was so prolonged that it wasn't to be taken until July 18th. He was with the Kent Regiment, the Buffs, and many years later was to relate his experiences. For some time his group were trapped in an ancient entrenchment with a line of hedges on a high bank in front of them and he described the sound of the bullets whistling over his head and the shredding of the branches above.

At the beginning of the Invasion of Europe the general public had no idea about the production in vast quantities of Hitler's latest weapon the first of his Vergeltungswaffen (Weapons of Revenge) and also the setting up of their launching sites. In the Spring of 1943 British Intelligence in London had been alerted by the Polish Resistance including a photograph sent from occupied Denmark. At least they knew of its existence but not when it would be deployed. Conventional bombing having ceased for us in Romford with the incendiaries on the night of 19th April 1944, we were then to be confronted with these new weapons which would shatter our nerves more than the Blitz.

VI

WEAPONS OF REVENGE

The VI Flying Bomb and the subsequent VII Rocket had been designed and developed by the German rocket propulsion scientist Dr. Werner von Braun at Usedem on the Baltic coast; the work eventually moving to Peenemunde also on the Baltic coast. Their production rate was 3,500 each month; some at the Vollkswagen factory, but this was interrupted by heavy bombing by the Allies. Costing £125 each and carrying a warhead weighing 2,000 lbs. they were to be launched from sloping ramps in the Pas de Calais area of France. Flying at 800-2000 ft. at 320-400 mph their throbbing pulse jet engines soon became a familiar sound and it is recorded that one was to fall on southern England every five minutes. The sound they made was a cross between a low flying helicopter and a two-stroke motorbike and they were nicknamed 'Buzz Bomb or 'Doodlebug'.

The first one in London on June 13th 1944 destroyed the railway bridge over Carpenter's Road just west of Stratford killing six and injuring nine people. The next morning Michael caught the 8.7 am from Romford station on his daily journey to Mercers School in Holborn. The train was diverted to Fenchurch Street and he didn't get to school until 12.30 pm. After lunch he was allowed to return home and from then on had a permanent late pass. It must have been a terrible job trying to establish some sort of timetable for the trains and the drivers had already had harrowing experiences during the Blitz. The boys who travelled by Tube had fewer problems. Mercers school was to be shut from June until the new term in September 1944 and the boys, class by class, went up for their exams, which were taken in the basement shelter. It was the year Michael's brother Peter took his Matric. exams.

We first heard the V1's the night of 15/16th June nine days after D-Day when a concentrated attack took place. It is recorded that 144 crossed the coast, 72 of which exploded in Greater London. Little information concerning the early ones leaked out and there were rumours of gas explosions as the authorities didn't want the Germans to know how close to the City they'd got. For us they were literally a rude awakening. We wondered what was happening as one by one we heard what sounded like an aircraft in trouble approaching, the engine cutting out and then an

107

explosion. We were so worried that they were our crippled aircraft trying to get back to Hornchurch aerodrome. Our nearest one that night exploded at Collier Row Road near Whalebone Lane and must have been near the Ack Ack gun site. We were soon to witness the damage they caused.

A chain of sirens sounded as they crossed the Kent coast and gun batteries there destroyed some whilst others flew on into the barrage balloons encircling London. Radar, already mentioned, could pick them up as they approached but their speed was such that there was little time to deal with them. In June 1944 Ack Ack guns from London had been moved to the North Downs in Kent, which I didn't know at the time. I remember the High School photograph taken in June 1944 before the end of term. This captured the cheerful optimism of some girls and the anxiety of others. I'm the solemn blonde in the front row above the 'TY' of 'COUNTY'.

COUNTY HIGH SCHOOL   FOR GIRLS, ROMFORD.
June   1944.

In July more 'Ack Ack' and 'Bofors' guns were moved to the coast in an endeavour to prevent some of VI's reaching their targets in the more densely populated areas inland. Their wingspan of 17ft meant they were difficult targets. Initially Spitfires, Mosquitos, Tempests, and Typhoons were used for combat but the VI's speed of just over 400 mph meant it was a very hazardous task. If they fired from too close their aircraft could be destroyed by the VI's exploding wreckage. HE lll German bombers were adapted to carry them attached beneath: their electrical release mechanism via an umbilical cord from the plane being cut off for their release. This enabled them to be transported nearer to their intended targets in and around London.

The one that landed in Hainault Road, Collier Row, Romford in the early hours of 20th June '44 caused a lot of damage. Three people were killed, eighteen seriously injured, some houses irreparably damaged and many properties including shops suffered badly. When I next visited Wendy in Linley Crescent the debris had been cleared and several houses in Hainault Road had tarpaulins draped over their roofs. Launchings were to continue until early October. Jeanne and I remember vividly the one which cleared the roof of our house as Mum approached the shelter with our boiled eggs in cups, one in each hand. Having yelled at her to "get down" she, bless her, lowered herself carefully balancing the eggcups. The engine of the growling doodlebug cut out and, after a moment's deadly silence, it exploded somewhere along Eastern Avenue behind us. We saw the back bedroom windows being sucked in by the blast and the sun glinting on them as they bulged back. We heard later that a passing motorist had been killed but there were no press details to give the full extent of damage and casualties. After this close encounter our Anderson shelter was re-sited opposite the kitchen door which meant more hard digging but we had quicker access if we needed to take cover. During one alert when my mother was preparing a meal I took our neighbour's dog into the shelter and cradled him in my arms as he was so scared. He knew what the siren meant and his acute hearing was on full alert for the sound of their approach.

During peaceful sessions in the summer I enjoyed gently drifting forward and back on the swing which Dad had set up for us and managed to read some of my homework text-books at the same time. I also improved my gymnastic skills by hanging like a bat from the overhead bar. This replenished the blood flow to my brain, but didn't do my mother's nerves much good! During winter alerts I did my homework sitting on the floor in the cupboard under the stairs, but it wasn't easy to 'drop a perpendicular' with my maths' exercise book propped on my thighs and map drawing was equally difficult. The time for handing in completed work was extended to a week but as I always tackled the ones I preferred first, I'd often spend most of the weekend completing the remainder!

Getting used to the V1's was like learning to ride a bike: we got a little better at it each day, but it was difficult not to wish they would pass us by as it meant others would suffer and I tried not to think about them as I concentrated on daily routine. In August 1944 the RAF fighters were to be joined by the Gloster Meteor I, the first operational jet. Since 1965 one of these was the mascot of Chelmsford's Air Cadets at their base in Meteor Way. Later it was to be refurbished and become a gate guardian at RAF

Leconfield. Pilots of the later Tempest V found that the turbulence from the upper surface of their wings when flying close under the wing of a V1 would cause it to tip and crash into the Channel before reaching the coast. Bomber Command too had been carrying out intensive raids on the V1's underground storage locations in northern France. An unexploded V1 was to be displayed in Romford Market in October 1944.

A Meteor

Remains of a V1 on a lorry in Romford Market

VII

ONCE MORE TO THE WEST

When schools broke up for the summer holidays it was decided that I should return to my grandparents in Somerset, but I was uneasy as I was loathe to leave the others in danger: Jeanne by that time being employed locally as a shorthand typist. Although approaching teenage I couldn't bear to leave my 'comforter' dog hanky case behind so he was washed, hung up to dry and given new button eyes to smarten him up. Mum took me to Paddington Station where I boarded the train and managed to get a corner seat so that we could talk until it left. A girl of similar age joined me, which pleased both mothers. At the last minute Richard Goolden, the BBC's, 'Night Watchman' climbed aboard placing his large suitcase precariously over our heads. After we suggested politely it might drop on us he tucked it under his legs. Mums with youngsters also boarded and the train was soon full. The whistle blew, my mother kissed me on the cheek and I waved from the window as the steam engine slowly tugged us away. To preserve her kiss I didn't wash that part of my face for weeks. I was grateful for the company of my new companion as far as Taunton where Aunt Em, down from Coventry for a break, met me and we boarded the Minehead train.

Gran and Grandad had by then moved to Liddimore Road Watchet. Aunt Phyl and Uncle Ray Bryant were nearby in Wyndham Road having moved there after their marriage in 1940. I was welcomed once more with much affection and almost the first thing I heard was the thudding of Ack Ack guns! A gunnery unit at nearby Doniford had regular target practice over the British Channel, the target being towed by a radio controlled de Havilland 'Queen Bee'. I was reassured by Gran that they didn't have air raids in Somerset. For a few nights I slept with cousin Vera as they'd had no time to get an extra single bed. The house in Watchet had a bathroom, main drains and electricity, which made life much easier for Gran and Grandad in their advancing years. They still had the same wireless set and its accumulator was collected each week for recharging at Williton. In the small garden at the back they kept chickens and the rooster woke us up early each morning. Excess eggs were preserved in isinglass in a bucket and Grandad kept a pig on his allotment not far away. He wore pebble glasses as his eyesight was failing badly with cataracts and seed packets were marked clearly in bold capitals for easy recognition.

Watchet Station

79 Liddimore Road

I soon settled in and familiarised myself with the local shops. Appropriately, the sweet shop was at Mr. and Mrs. Tucker's house nearby. Soon after I'd settled in Gran and I went by train to an auction at Minehead where she managed to get a corner wardrobe to accommodate the extra clothes. I'd never been to one before and when I spotted a small glass brass lidded inkwell in a box of oddments I asked an attendant how much it was. He looked very kindly at me, asked if I had a pocket and popped it in. Although I hadn't actually asked for it because I had been taught not to, I had pangs of conscience about accepting it. Gran and I managed to manoeuvre all the purchases alongside us for the return journey. At Blue Anchor some London mums with children in tow were repelled by Gran who, with arms crossed on the lowered window ledge replied "There's no more room in here" to which one of the mums retorted "She's brought 'er bl**din ticket and thinks she's brought the bl**din train". They must have been under a lot of strain being away from home with the responsibility of young ones and I felt sorry for them. Deciding to remain neutral, I lowered my gaze, slid down in the seat and tried very hard to keep a straight face! Gran's tactics were successful, but unfortunately when she resumed her seat she sat on our meat pies and it amused Grandad when he was presented with a pancaked one for his tea!

I visited Aunt Phyl and Uncle Ray when they were at home but they were fully occupied most of the time. He often worked overtime at weekends at the BBC at Washford and, as they had no children of their own or evacuees, Aunt Phyl was obliged to take a job. This was in the upper part of a ramshackle building to the rear of the present Post Office in Swain Street where they made metal components for tanks. Not having been issued with adequate protection, a minute particle of metal in her eye made her seek alternative employment and she became a shop assistant for a local grocer. Some evenings with a young helper she worked as projectionist at the Conquest cinema, which fronted the promenade. Will Hay and Laurel & Hardy films were among the popular ones. Aunt Phyl said that on occasions things became a bit hectic when the celluloid film caught fire. The flames had to be doused and she soon became adept at splicing the film before "normal service could be resumed as soon as possible!" Uncle Ray prepared coloured celluloid advertising slides for the interval with copperplate handwritten slogans. Music was played whilst they were shown and iced water lollipops sold to the audience. I am sure they rose to sing the National Anthem at the end; a custom which has long since vanished in the mists of time.

The Conquest Cinema

West Somerset Hotel

Other evenings Bertha Hooper appreciated Aunt Phyl and Uncle Ray's help at the West Somerset Hotel as her husband Len was a Captain in the army and not on leave very often. They were always busy and members of the United States Army Air Corps based at St. Audries were amongst their customers. They had a "Harvard" trainer plane and Aunt Phyl has told me she accepted the offer of a flight with one of them, but when he flew out over the Bristol Channel she told him to get her back as she couldn't swim. After landing she enquired why he had a bandage over his forehead and he replied "I crashed on Exmoor yesterday!"

I soon became firm friends with Bertha's daughter Susanne who was glad to get out and about during the summer holiday. Although five years younger than me we bridged the gap easily and, with a packet of sandwiches apiece, would spend the whole day out enjoying visits to West beach to look for alabaster or perhaps a walk up the mineral line inland. On the cliff tops east of the harbour we picked up pieces of shredded red target cloth from the gunnery practise sessions. The gunners were almost certainly from a Scottish regiment as I remember, whilst waiting for a bus one morning, a cheery group of them entertaining the queue with a hearty rendition of "I belong to Glasgy, dear ole Glasgy toon"! The bus stop next to the station was across from the milk bar, which was a popular venue.

West Beach

One day Gran agreed to provide bed and breakfast for two men who knocked at the door. I think they must have been Austrian Jews as they spoke German and were perhaps internees who had been were released in 1942. They had violins and told us they were members of the New London Symphony Orchestra. Because live Promenade Concerts had

115

been cancelled at this time and were broadcast instead, perhaps they had come to the west country for some respite? They were very polite and each morning dipped their heads and greeted me with "Guten morgen mein fraulein". I replied with "….mein herr" and regretted that I was learning Latin instead of German as I enjoyed talking to people and loved to learn about other people's experiences.

Sometimes on Sunday afternoons I'd walk down to the promenade to listen to the Watchet Town band playing in the bandstand: the latter has since been dismantled and a statue of Taylor Coleridge's 'The Ancient Mariner' is nearby. When the tide was out the harbour was thick mud and I remember the panic when a boy fell off the slipway and wallowed frantically until someone grabbed him to safety. On other occasions, on the incoming tide, it was interesting to watch the ships docking and unloading coal from the Welsh mines and reloading with timber for pit props for the return journey. Other ships came from Spain with esparto grass for processing at Watchet Paper Mill. The dockside crane was kept busy loading and unloading the goods trucks on the adjacent siding from the station. At Timberscombe I wouldn't have had these interesting diversions and they did help to pass the time.

The Harbour

My grandparents told me that if the Welsh coast was very clear it meant rain was on the way and this has always happened. We visit west Somerset at regular intervals and I always look across the channel to check pending weather conditions. The harbour now is full of pleasure craft but in 1944 I remember the local boats bringing in regular catches.

Gran asked me one day to bring home some sprats from the fishmonger in Anchor Street for a snack and Grandad watched with amusement as I carefully filleted each one before eating it! On other occasions I took the train to Blue Anchor to spend time on the beach and I remember the waiting room walls covered with Americans' signatures. I know now that they were not allowed to drink prior to going into action. Before the Normandy landings they had been conspicuous by their absence at the West Somerset Hotel bar and Uncle Ray had commented on it. Some locals have recalled how they had heard them leaving their camp at St. Audries very quietly in the early hours of the following morning and without leaving any traces of their occupation. From there they must have headed to the beaches of south Devon ready for the long awaited invasion on Tuesday 6th June 1944. Their camp at St Audries is now a caravan and camping site. They probably obtained their water from the fresh water spring nearby and local folklore has suggested this was also used at night when crew members of U-boats patrolling the Bristol Channel came ashore for fresh supplies, but I don't know if this is true.

One day on West beach cousin Vera and I met some American servicemen who were recuperating from the Normandy landings. Their encampment was on the cliffs to the east of Watchet Harbour: much of this area has since crumbled into the sea. Having seen TV coverage of their landings on the Utah and particularly Omahah beaches, plus reading about the consequences of subsequent military action, I have a clearer idea of their experiences. During the period mid June to mid July, the number of their fatalities trebled to over 10,500 and the wounded trebled to over 50,000. This, coupled with Uncle Ern's experiences, makes me appreciate how glad they must have been to be getting back to some form of normality for a while when we met them.

They were very polite and introduced themselves as Lou and Al. I know now that they had been issued with a booklet on how to behave when in Britain. Some people classified them as "over-dressed, over-sexed and over here", but to us they were just two nice Americans who wanted to chat for a while. We searched for flat pebbles to play 'Ducks and Drakes' and they achieved much better results. I still wonder where their homes were and whether they returned safely. They weren't many years older than me and I felt very sorry for them: they were much further away from home than I was and must have been missing their families as much as I did mine. One day I watched a boxing tournament which they held at the recreation ground. This helped to keep them fit and also fostered good relations with the locals.

As time progressed and the early corn was harvested, Susanne and I were given permission to glean the residue from the corner of a field for

Gran's chickens and also pick up early windfalls from an orchard for Grandad's pig. Rival their Pembrokeshire corgi was still with them. He was getting old and needed carrying back when I took him for walks. Corgis are lengthy dogs and he needed supporting with both my arms in front, which was exhausting! I felt sorry for both of us and the walks got shorter to make things easier. When eventually he died he was buried in Grandad's allotment as he'd had fireworks thrown at him when younger which made him terrified of fire. Grandad was very kind and caring and decided not to take him to be incinerated at the Gasworks.

Sometimes I went to the beach on my own. I was still so worried about the safety of the family back home as I had seen the terrible damage caused by the V1's before I left. I hadn't any photos of them and would lie on the beach with my eyes shut trying to picture their dear faces. I couldn't telephone them as we had to wait until 1948 to get one and mobile phones hadn't been invented. I needed so much to have a reassuring chat to hear they were alright. Outwardly I managed to keep reasonably cheerful, but when I received a short letter from Jeanne that finished with "must stop now as the siren has just gone" I couldn't stop thinking they may have been killed since she'd posted it. Gran and Grandad must have been worried too, but he set aside his newspaper, sat me on his knee and tried to distract me with tales of his amusing experiences with horses whilst in the Veterinary Corps in WWI. They were exercised in the sea and on one occasion he had slid round the horse and ended up clinging to it upside down under water!

My fears wouldn't go away and one morning I broke down and couldn't stop crying. Aunt Emmie, on a visit from Coventry, suggested I should visit Gran's Dr. Collins. He was very understanding, asked me where I came from and talked of a visit he'd paid to Romford. I think most of what he said went over my head, as I was so distraught. By then we were nearing the start of the autumn term and arrangements were to have been made for me to attend Minehead High School for Girls and live with Aunt Bessie Passmore at Alcombe. Normally I would have been delighted as Jeanne and I had always enjoyed time spent with cousin Gerry on holidays, but this was different and I felt the same as I had at Timberscombe in 1940 and couldn't be persuaded. It was selfish of me as my family knew that at least one of us would be safe. My mother was contacted and travelled down to take me back by coach. Unfortunately it broke down near Salisbury Plain and we had to wait some time for a relief to pick us up.

VIII

ROVER'S RETURN

Whilst I'd been in Somerset I had been trying hard to take one day at a time and rarely looked at newspapers, but at home I was more aware of current events. By lst September 1944 the Allied advances across Europe had enabled them eventually to cross the river Seine. It was then that General Eisenhower, Supreme Allied Commander in Europe, was given the role of Ground Force Commander in North West Europe and Montgomery became a Field Marshall. More doodlebugs had landed in Essex whilst I was in Somerset and were to continue until November. Their launchings were to be overlapped by an even more frightening weapon, the V2 rocket.

V2 Rocket

Our nerves had been shattered enough by the V1's but the V2 Rockets were to be far worse. Measuring about 45 ft. long and 6 ft. wide with a warhead weighing a ton, they cost £6,000 each to produce. Developing a sonic speed of 3,600 mph, about a mile a second, they reached a height of 55-60 miles before descending to the ground with an impact speed of over

2,500 mph. They only took just over four minutes to cover the distance of around one hundred and ninety miles to reach us; about the time it takes to boil an egg but not quite as fast as Roger Bannister's record breaking four minute mile. The first for Essex from the Hague on the Dutch coast landed in a field at Noak Hill on 16th September 1944 a week after my thirteenth birthday.

Having returned to High school I was in the third year where our form room was on the first floor and the fact that we were a long way from the shelters was no longer relevant as we wouldn't have had time to reach them. It was the year we began Physics which was to present me with yet another challenge, but we were luckier than the girls in the upper forms who were cramming for their forthcoming School and Higher School certificates. Continuity of study was interrupted at times as staff came and went and having more than one Latin teacher didn't help as I had struggled with it from the start. Also, around this time, my mother had coaxed me into starting a course of orthodontic treatment to straighten my front teeth. Although reluctant to take on anything else I visited Mr. Norris in Eastern Road who was so reassuring that I agreed to it.

Rocket attacks were to continue and Ian Hook, Keeper of the Essex Regiment Museum, told us that Hylands House Chelmsford was the HQ for 1 SAS from May '44 prior to D-Day until disbandment in '46. During the V2 period he believes, for interest during rest periods, they may well have watched the re-entry of some of the rockets into the earth's atmosphere. A TV programme mentioned that agents in Belgium sent information of the launch sites. Unfortunately for us, in spite of constant bombing raids by Bomber Command, the V2's were 'moveable beasts' as they and their launching pads could be transported easily to new sites as the Allies advanced. We did have some 'light' relief when on 17th September the 'Blackout' was suspended and replaced by a 'Dimout' which increased the intensity of light permitted.

The Dimout coincided with the dropping of troops for the for the Battle of Arnhem and, at the Army Air Corps museum at Middle Wallop in Hampshire, they have extensive displays depicting the courage and determination of those involved in airborne operations. The length of the Horsa glider body is 67ft, just over the length of a cricket pitch, and the wing span also. It carried twenty-nine passengers and there were two pilots: the latter being trained to the same fighting capacity. It resembles a giant pea pod and, looking into the dim interior, I can only imagine what it must have been like for the men sitting inside with equipment strapped, pocketed, and hung on them whilst awaiting take-off and the hazards ahead. The Combined Military Services Museum at Maldon in Essex has a model of a paratrooper dressed and equipped with all the necessary gear. Two working colleagues of Michael in the 1950's had been involved in the raid; one an RAF pilot and the other a parachutist.

In 1988 whilst looking up details of the 'Armada' at the Public Record Office in Chancery Lane, I spotted an adjacent file on "Arnhem" and amongst its contents was a scrap of paper with the message "They knew we were coming". The message gave food for thought but I have only recently read more about the course of events at that time. Operation Market Garden began on Sunday morning 17th September '44, which was the day after the first V2 had landed in our area. The bridge at Arnhem was the target with 10,000 British 1st Airborne and 2,400 Polish Para Brigade being parachuted or glider-landed behind enemy lines.

The opening of sluice gates by the Germans having flooded the area meant digging trenches became a futile task. Bad weather soaked and muddied the troops, their small arms malfunctioned and inadequate radio equipment failed. They were met with strong resistance by two SS Panzer Divisions and one report reveals that plans for the operation were found on a captured Allied officer whose glider had been shot down. Subsequent support vehicles had difficulty in negotiating the approach road as one slip would have tipped them into the irrigation ditches. Having fought valiantly for nearly ten days the troops were forced to withdraw on 26th September and were taken prisoner with both sides suffering substantial losses.

The Germans in the meantime were continuing their V2 launchings from alternative sites and these were to continue until 26th March 1945. Official news of them was released eventually by the Germans on the 8th November 1944 and this was followed by an announcement by Churchill in the Commons with the Press and Radio giving brief details. There would be no warning of their approach and no time for us to take evasive action. They didn't mention radar, of course, because of security: this could detect the V2's but there was no time to warn the general public. The complete knowledge of their capabilities was a frightening prospect as a lot of us were so tired with coping with all that had happened since 1939. We had been at war over five years and by then I had become a teenager. Adolescence can be a stressful time under normal circumstances but with this new threat I don't mind admitting that I was really scared and wondered how I would cope.

I remember the V2 that landed at the junction of Rosedale Road and Collier Row Lane early on the 16th November 1944. I was sitting on the loo when the landing lino rose up like a flying carpet and settled back. On my way to catch the 247 bus to school the walking wounded were filing quietly across the arterial road for treatment at the first-aid post at the rear of the Parkside Hotel, now called 'The Squire'. Some had bandaged heads and others had arms in slings. Dad walked later to Linley Crescent to see if Wendy and her mother Edna were all right. Both their front and back doors had been blown open and they had damage to their house, but fortunately they had been in their shelter. After the area of debris was cleared Wendy and her mother were able to walk directly across the wasteland to the shops in Collier Row. It was to be considered the worst incident in Romford; twenty-one houses being demolished, thirteen people killed and thirty-two badly injured. Amongst those killed were Blanche Larner the wife of one of Dad's colleagues at the substation and also Betty Mitchell and her mother Lillian. Betty didn't arrive at Romford station that morning to travel to London as usual with Jeanne.

It wasn't long after that incident that dad brought home a bicycle and a hockey stick without revealing their origin, but I think the bicycle must have belonged to Blanche. I did overhear him say that someone had been thrown onto the fire they were sitting by to keep warm on what was a chilly morning, which caused their death. Dad serviced the bike and I began cycling to school. Bus passes weren't to be issued until 1946 and I enjoyed cycling in spite of the weight of books and sports equipment. After a close encounter with two double decker buses travelling in opposite directions in Romford town centre I took a route via Pettits Lane, Junction Road and the footbridge over the railway. Soon tiring of manhandling the bike and all my school impedimenta over the bridge I chose a much longer route via the Arterial, Heath Park Road, Balgores Lane and Brentwood Road via The Drill.

One morning on the Arterial, I was delayed by an endless convoy of buses and coaches requisitioned for reinforcement troop transportation, which was heading for the coast. Pre-War we had watched coach loads of Londoners with children clutching buckets and spades and waving flags out of the windows in eager anticipation. The servicemen I saw were on a more serious mission but were still cheerful. One of them poked his smiley face and a hand through a fanlight shouting "Can you post this for me love?" With a quick smile and "yes" from me and "thanks" from him the letter plus stamp money wrapped in a scrap of paper landed neatly at my feet. He had probably avoided statutory censorship by doing this. Having retrieved them I watched the convoy dwindling until it disappeared and couldn't help wondering what would happen to them all. I wanted an end to the VII's but didn't want them to suffer. I noticed the envelope had a London address and would willingly have provided the stamp.

Before Christmas Wendy and I were involved in rehearsals for the panto Aladdin, I had increased homework to do and the VII's continued. The one that affected me most plunged deep into allotments near

Elmhurst Drive off Osborne Road to the rear of the High School. It was during lunch break on Friday 1st December 1944 and I was alone in the cloakroom changing into my outdoor shoes. The sequence of events was rapid. For an n'th of a second the light was blotted out at the window and a whooshing sound was followed by an explosion nearby. Seconds later a second bang was followed by a sound like a strong wind in a storm gusting against windows. It was my first experience of a sonic boom as the V2 re-entered the earth's atmosphere. I didn't like Physics and this demonstration of 'Rocket science' was too close for comfort.

The Assembly Hall

Needing human contact I knew I had to get out and hurried through the empty assembly hall and deserted corridors hoping nothing would collapse on me and I'd be found if it did. I was so relieved when I found my classmates amongst the 'rugby scrums' assembled on the playing fields discussing the incident. The complement of about five hundred girls and thirty plus staff had reacted with speed and the evacuation drill had worked well. It was fortunate that the V2 had landed on the allotments as concrete surfaces produced more devastation. Some houses were damaged and thirty-three people slightly injured. After school I cycled to Salisbury Road School for a charity concert, which helped to take my mind off the event. My mother who had brought my costumes was anxiously awaiting my arrival as she had been told the area in which it had landed.

The School Playing Fields

This was a period of 'ups and downs' and a much less serious problem had to be dealt with. Export of rubber from Malaysia having ceased with the Japanese occupation, supplies for elastic plummeted and so did our under garments! We either had to knot them at the waist or use safety pins to retain our dignity in public. The pins weren't always reliable and a delayed response to a 'call of nature' meant clutching our clothing whilst trying to hobble cross-legged to the loo. Thank goodness we were an 'all girl' school! We swapped stories about our experiences, which helped ease our underlying tension. Things were to be no better post-war two years later when, at the SEETC (South East Essex Technical College) at Barking, I witnessed our English mistress stepping neatly out of hers to scoop them up before entering the staff room! Trousers were worn by women in the Land Army and those working in factories etc. and would have been much more practical for us.

The public were trying to 'take it' but when conditions deteriorated it was more like our winter of 'despair' rather than 'discontent'. The winter of 1944/45 was one of the worst on record in England with food and fuel still strictly rationed. Freeing the frozen outlet pipes from our bathroom wash basin and kitchen sink had to be tackled and I remember one morning before school perching perilously on a step ladder on icy ground with a jug of hot water to help clear the upper one with my hands freezing in the process. It must have been a difficult time for mums with husbands away in the Forces and having to cope alone. Allied bombing missions from East Anglia to Germany were hampered also by snow, ice and freezing fog and it must have been a great challenge to the crews involved.

Conditions became so bad I had to give up cycling to school and, with all my school gear hoisted around me, took to the bus. These had female 'Clippies' or older male conductors and one morning I was barred from boarding by a male with a curt announcement "workers first". Mentally classifying him as a 'Little Hitler', a popular term for over zealous uniformed workers at the time, I lowered my gear to the ground to await the next bus which gave me time to rationalise that he was probably stressed and only carrying out orders. I missed roll call and was rebuked by my form mistress as it was essential to know who was present before we dispersed for lessons. The snow also presented another problem, when for about three mornings I was pelted with snowballs by several Pettits Lane schoolgirls going in the opposite direction. I was ready for them the next morning hunkered under our privet hedge with a ready-made pile of snowballs alongside which I launched as they drew level. A tacit truce was acknowledged and from then on we exchanged smiles instead of snowy missiles!

Christmas and the pantomime Aladdin came and went and I decided finally to give up dancing to concentrate on school work. The drooping of a badly hung side curtain whilst making a quick change of costume during a performance at St. Edwards School resulted in my involuntary strip tease act. Like spectators at Wimbledon the eyes of the audience alternated between my struggles to get into a acrobat bikini and the action on stage and I had to go back on within a few moments. This was the moment I made my decision!

Early 1945 was one of general uncertainty. British bombers were targeting places in Germany and on the night of 13/14th February 1945 Dresden suffered badly. Ralph Hyams of Parkside Avenue was on that mission, was shot down, taken prisoner and not released until the end of the war. Coverage of the incident reports that the fires could be seen two hundred miles away and thousands of civilians were incinerated. We weren't happy about what was happening to us with the V2's, but this was a terrible experience for the occupants in Dresden that night which apparently included refugees from the Russian Front; the estimated total of those killed numbering 80,000. Eventually we were to learn that more civilians had died that night than in the whole of the Blitz on London when about 40,000 civilians were killed.

The atomic bomb to be dropped on Hiroshima on the morning of 6th August 1945 was to cause an initial death toll of 71,879 which, although less than Dresden, was equally horrific. In 2010, the sixty-fifth anniversary of the event, the memories of the survivors were still haunting them and I am so grateful that Hitler's intentions to use the V2 rocket to carry nuclear weapons hadn't materalised due to the activities of the Norwegian saboteurs in 1943.

During the evening of 20th February 1945 a V2 landed about half a mile from the High School in the back gardens of Fairholme Avenue bordering the railway line. Seven houses were affected and twelve people were killed including my dentist Mr. Norris who had been visiting friends. The loss of two fingers on his left hand in an earlier shooting accident enabled them to establish his identity. I was only about halfway through my orthodontic treatment and had built up so much confidence with him and suddenly he had gone and it wasn't a good time for me to get used to another.

The V2 which fell on Smithfield on 8th March was in close proximity to Mercers school in Holborn. Michael and his classmates were in the playground at break time when it landed. All the windows were blown out and shards of glass and debris littered the playground, but miraculously not one of the boys was hurt. This V2 was devastating as it landed whilst people were queuing for rabbits at the market nearby to supplement their rations and tragically over a hundred people were killed. It took some time to locate the victims as it had penetrated into the underground railway. Cousin Geoffrey Prole has told us that a colleague of his, who drove Royal Blue coaches to London from Somerset during the war, used to fill the luggage hold with rabbits. On arrival at the terminus the queue for them was longer than that for coaches. People including chefs from hotels were willing to pay 2/6d. each for them.

Early morning on the 12th March 1945 yet another V2 landed in Hylands Park Hornchurch adjoining the playing fields at the back of the High School. On our arrival we were allowed to collect as many relevant text books as possible for study at home. We approached our form room on the first floor to the rear of the building with caution as it was in the area most affected. The full structural survey, clearance and necessary repairs gave us five weeks for the Easter holiday. On a visit to the school in 2009, kindly arranged by Rosemary Gaughan the Deputy Headmistress, our guide Nelson Amoah told us that they had discovered a pit on the perimeter of the playing field containing a large quantity of broken glass so maybe it was the shattered glass from that incident? It could have been the location of the underground shelters or the school allotments in which we 'Dug for Victory' weekdays and at weekends. This was to continue after the war as food was so short.

To return to military operations in Europe at that time, the Middle Wallop Army Air Corps Museum also gives details of Operation Varsity which took place on 24th March '45, its objective being the eventual crossing of the Rhine the last major obstacle before the Allies could reach

Berlin. It was the largest airborne operation in history and involved British, Canadian and American forces and the people living near the south coast must have had a wonderful view of the mass of planes that crossed the Channel. The troops were flown in Commando transporters and gliders, 'Skytrain' planes and supported by fighters and I have only just read that Winston Churchill witnessed their final approach to the target. Eventually they were to link up with Allied ground forces. Twenty-four hours later the Allies' mission was accomplished but with heavy losses: 1,111 died, 1,625 were wounded and 50 aircraft and 11 gliders shot down. It must have been a nerve-racking experience for those who took part. A glider trooper who absented himself because of a premonition had his sentence reduced as, in the event, his glider had been destroyed with no survivors. I know I would have found it very difficult and have the greatest admiration for the tremendous effort and sacrifice of all the men who took part on our behalf.

Meanwhile the launching of V2s continued and on 26th March 1945 the "venturi", compulsion unit of one, plunged into the garden waste heap in Mrs. Payne's back garden at 94 Parkside Avenue diagonally opposite us. It was in the evening when most people were at home and neighbours filed through to view it. Resembling a large inverted metal cauldron with a conical base it was extremely hot after its journey through space and was fast-forwarding the composting process which we could smell as we approached. The lethal warhead had gone on to land on the corner of Mawney Road and Forest Road where it destroyed sixteen houses, killed two people and thirty-four were taken to hospital. That was to be the last V2 in our vicinity and about four hours later the last in Havering, like the first some six months earlier, landed in the Noak Hill area. Having caused damage over a wide area to a total of 1.25 million homes, three days later on 29th March they were at last withdrawn out of range into Germany. Later statistics were to reveal that nearly four hundred had landed in Essex, Hornchurch receiving thirty-nine and Romford twenty-two.

We didn't know at the time that the V2 rocket was capable of carrying a nuclear weapon. Successive attempts by the Allies had been made to destroy the heavy water plant at Vemork in Norway and in early 1943 Norwegian members of the SOE had finally succeeded in Operation Gunnerside. This was to be considered the major sabotage act of WWII. After subsequent Allied bombing raids, attempts by the Germans to remove the remaining heavy water to Germany via Lake Tinnsjo failed when the ferry boat was sunk by the Resistance. If they hadn't suceeded we would have been subjected to attacks by an even more lethal weapon.

Venturi

After our extended Easter holiday caused by the V2 on 12th March we returned to High School around the middle of April '45 and resumed our studies. Although food supplies were still limited we managed, but because they were so low in Europe the Germans asked for help to feed the thousands of people who were starving and a temporary cease-fire was arranged for the RAF to drop relief supplies somewhere in Holland. Although we had not suffered nearly so much, by then we were desperate for the war to end and the weeks seemed to drag. Hitler reached his 56th birthday on 20th April and when news of his suicide was announced ten days later I hope I can be forgiven for being relieved: I am ashamed also to admit that I had been disappointed when the plot for his assasination had failed on 20th July 1944. After marrying his mistress Ava Braun on 29th April 1945, the following day they committed joint suicide in his bunker when he shot her and then took a suicide pill. With Russian troops advancing it was decided that their bodies should be burned. Admiral Doenitz took over command and hostilities came to an end with the signing of the Unconditional Surrender at Rheims on 7th May 1945. After confusion about when news of this should be disclosed, a public holiday was announced for Tuesday the 8th.

Damage at Mawney Road

IX

VE CELEBRATIONS

It was decided that Dad, Jeanne and I would go to London to celebrate, but Mum said she knew she would tire sooner than us. We went by train to Liverpool Street and made our way to Buckingham Palace where, as we were among the early arrivals, we managed to get a position within the railings encircling Buckingham Palace. This meant we weren't pressed from the rear and I could scramble onto the low support wall if necessary. Here we had a clear view of the balcony and settled down to wait. The military band played with intervals of rest until insistent calls of "We want the King" got them playing once more: the Royal Air Force march is the one I remember most. Eventually we were packed so tight that I couldn't raise my arms from my sides, had to stand on tiptoe to see and took advantage of the support wall. Each time the Royal Family came out the cheering was deafening and when Winston Churchill appeared with his salute it swelled again.

After the final appearance on the balcony we made our way to Waterloo Bridge, clamping our arms across each others' backs to keep together. I would have been so scared if we had been separated. We managed to get places at the parapet of the bridge and watched the biggest firework display we had ever witnessed. Magnificent set pieces, which must have taken ages to assemble, were in position along the riverside and, looking skywards, we could see all the myriad rockets as they were launched. As they soared into the sky so did our jubilant spirits. The unhurried surface of the Thames reflected the sparkling extravaganza of multi-coloured lights so it was a double delight. After the final display puttered to an end and the gasps of appreciation subsided, we leaned over the parapet to watch an endless armada of spent rocket sticks floating through the arches beneath us to make their way eastwards. So many weapons of war had come to London in the opposite direction, but these rockets were friendly and now at last it was all over.

Eventually we made our way to Liverpool Street station. Dad, having been born and raised in London, knew every part of the City well and, as we made our way back via the Embankment and Temple Gardens, he told us how his parents used to take him as a child to listen to the brass bands

130

playing at the bandstand there. The streets were packed with jubilant crowds the whole way and somehow we managed to keep together. Jeanne remembers our desperate dash to the loo when we reached Liverpool Street as we were bursting to 'spend a penny'. We caught the last train at about 12.30 p.m. and at Romford, as there were no buses running, we had to walk over a mile home to Parkside Avenue. Not surprisingly we were tired when we got home but told Mum about the excitement of it all. It was around two o'clock when we fell into our beds exhausted but exhilarated and slept soundly knowing there would be no more sirens, we wouldn't have to drag ourselves out of bed at a moment's notice and there would be no more unheralded rockets hurtling down from the sky. The poem 'The Great Lover' written by WWI poet Rupert Brooke reflects how I felt. We would be able to have a good night's sleep with the 'cool kindliness of sheets that soon smooth away trouble', beneath 'the rough male kiss of blankets' and enjoy the luxury of a bath any time with 'the benison of hot water', without interruption. After five years and eight months the relief for us was overwhelming, but many families were still awaiting news of their loved ones still fighting in the Far East.

Many houses in our street were decorated with flags and bunting for the celebrations. Ours had been languishing in the loft since the Coronation of King George VI and Queen Elizabeth in 1937. The party, which was held alongside the bugalows at the botton of Parkside Avenue, was a great success. A piano was brought out for entertainment and competitive races held. Leslie Sarone, one of the 'Two Leslies' judged the Fancy Dress competition. I wore an old panto Guard's outfit and, with an empty McKintosh sweet tin, represented Quality Street and Michael portrayed the Duke of Wellington. I didn't know then we were to be married on the 18th June 1955, the 140th anniversary of the Battle of Waterloo! Refreshments provided by the mums were at the parade of shops at Rise Park Boulevard in the shell of an incomplete shop.

After the euphoria of the celebrations we had to settle down to continued rationing which was to go on for some time. Potatoes and bread were added to the rations and I remember Wendy and I collecting the coupons from the Main Road Food Office. When sweets were finally to come off ration they were 'hoovered up' immediately by endless queues: I remember the ones at Maynards in the Arcade near the Market in Romford. Because of the demand they were rationed again. Fresh eggs in 1953 and meat in 1954 were to be the last items to be released, the latter being a year before our wedding in 1955.

At High School at the beginning of 1945 I was in the third year, which was considered the least demanding for workload, and it was decided we should stage a mimed version of Peter Pan, with the choir providing the narrative. Because I was the smallest I was given the part of Peter and Gwen Tupman was Wendy. Sporting fixtures were to begin again with other schools and I played in a rounders team in the summer and hockey in the winter.

Day to day life soon became routine and the War for us in England slipped into the background. Our biggest shock was to be the landslide defeat of Winston Churchill who was replaced by Clement Atlee as our new Prime Minister. It was hard to take in after all that Churchill had achieved on our behalf.

In August 1945 we were to be shocked once more by the news of the atomic bomb dropped on Hiroshima on the 6th followed by the one on Nagasaki on the 9th, which brought the war in the Far East back into sharp focus. At Romford Main Road Baptist church in the early 1950s we were to be visited and given a talk by Dr. Kagawa about the bombing. The church was packed to full capacity with chairs in the aisles and people sitting on the stairs in the gallery. So many people wanted to hear him and it was a very emotional gathering. He said that the adverse weather conditions meant the bombs had been dropped on Japan's strongest Christian locations and he was so sad. We all know the devastating effect they had and the repercussions, which were to continue for so long. Although we had all wanted the War to end we felt so sorry for the civilians who had to suffer for it finally to happen. It must have been a desperate decision for President Truman to make and his comment "The buck stops here" is recorded in history.

The terrible experiences of our servicemen who were Japanese prisoners of war were equally harrowing, many of whom were unable to recount them until much later. A lot of them felt as if they were 'The Forgotten Army'. Lord Louis Mountbatten did his very best to get them out and also the servicemen still in the Burmese jungle back to England as soon as possible. David Capps the husband of Michael's cousin Dorothy was amongst them. There were difficulties in tracing many and the injured needed treatment before repatriation. Uncle Ern who was in Bombay with the Medical Corps, probably in a transit camp, must have been involved. He didn't get back to England until the end of June/beginning July 1946. He told us about the extreme heat in India: if he had a cold drink it broke out immediately in sweat and poured down his face. He did, however, enjoy the magnificent scenery when they moved up into the foothills.

Len Clark, a neighbour of Michael's parents in Lodge Avenue, recounted his experiences in a Japanese POW camp. He kept himself occupied making shorts for his fellow prisoners with any material he could lay his hands on, using a needle he fashioned out of an old bicycle spoke. The latrine at his camp was a plank over a river and he told us that, when he suffered a bout of dysentry necessitating frequent trips, another prisoner was always there. When he sympathised with him he was told that he was fishing for something to eat. The Japanese soldiers had been taught that surrender was dishonourable and despised their prisoners. The heat must have been intolerable and we have learned that in some camps the POW's were forced to stand out in it.

Many years after the War, David Capps the husband of Michael's cousin Dorothy, was to relate his experiences with the Royal Kent Regiment who were involved in the decisive battle of El Alamein, the advance through North Africa and then into Sicily and Italy. Returning home they sailed on D-Day+1 and were holed up during the battle for Caen: mentioned earlier. They were pulled back on the way to the German border and told they were to be on escort duty to India, but on arrival were sent up the Burmese jungle. Although he had a two-figure demob' number it was to take a fortnight to get his group out of the jungle and, of the original 1,000 members of his regiment, he was one of the seven comparatively unscathed at the end. He told us that after three serious engagements they became 'combat wise' with more chance of survival. He and Dorothy were to be allotted one of the pre-fabs in Collier Row. He went on fishing trips with friends which gave him time to 'step aside' and he also won prizes for his garden. He was a quiet and undemonstrative person and one of the thousands of unsung heroes.

A Prefab

The repatriation of Prisoners of War on both sides was to take some time and Michael remembers the Germans in a camp at Harold Hill near Romford who were employed in post-war reconstruction work. The minister of Main Road Baptist Church 'VJ' Smith suggested the Young People's Fellowship should extend hands of friendship to them. They were invited to the Young People's Fellowship meetings and also Sunday services. Several responded and attended them wearing dark uniforms with a diamond shaped mark on the back. Michael remembers practising his German on them. Some of the young people, with their parents' consent, invited them to their homes. It was a very thoughtful gesture by VJ and for several years at Christmas and Easter grateful greetings were received from ex-prisoner Adolph Conrad. The German POW's who were 'anti-Stalin' had been reluctant to return. This was another difficult decision for Churchill to make, as he was naturally anxious to get our own POW's back from Eastern Europe.

The Y.P.F. with Prisoners of War.

German POWs & the Y.P.F.

EPILOGUE

Reconciliation is heartening after conflict and continuing friendship and communication to keep up the bonds of peace so important. The 100th anniversary of the founding of the Scout movement was held at Hylands Park in Chelmsford with around 40,000 youngsters from all over the world attending. From a vantage point at Widford we looked down on them living together in peace and harmony and enjoyed the sound of drums that floated up to us. We watched them queuing to register their names and countries of origin on strips of paper to be joined together in a long ribbon. The words on the BBC crest came into mind 'Nation shall speak peace unto Nation'. We felt Chelmsford was an appropriate place as it is the birthplace of communication, the first sound broadcast having been made in June 1920.

The site when vacated was completely free of litter and the only signs of occupancy the faded patches of grass where their tents had been. It was good to have seen the ones who made trips into town, particularly the young Germans in Backnang Square where the twinning sculpture was sited in 1990. We have no ill feelings towards them and I am sure the majority of their forebears as servicemen and civilians hadn't wanted the war any more than we did. The youngsters of today are our ambassadors for the future and now, with satellite technology, the opportunities of communication are endless for them all to keep in touch.

Backnang sculpture

The Dresden Cross

Some years ago Jeanne and our nephew Mark, who live in Coventry, took us to the cathedral to see the cross to be presented to the citizens of Dresden for the top of their cathedral as an act of reconciliation. On 14th November 1990 a hand bell, inscribed in English and German, was presented to HM Queen Mother by the President of the Federal Republic of Germany during the service of Remembrance and Reconciliation on the 50th anniversary of the bombing of Coventry. In the grounds of the cathedral is a sculpture 'Reconciliation' donated by Richard Branson. In 1995 a copy of this was to be presented by the citizens of Coventry to Hiroshima to be placed in their 'Garden of Peace'.

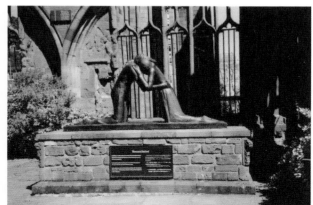

The Bell and the Hiroshima Sculpture at Coventry

On the first anniversary of VE day, on 8th June 1946, King George VI sent a personal message of thanks to the schoolchildren of England thanking them for their contribution and efforts, the message ending with 'May these qualities be yours as you grow up and join in the common effort to establish among the nations of the world unity and peace.'

8th June, 1946

To-day, as we celebrate victory, I send this personal message to you and all other boys and girls at school. For you have shared in the hardships and dangers of a total war and you have shared no less in the triumph of the Allied Nations.

I know you will always feel proud to belong to a country which was capable of such supreme effort; proud, too, of parents and elder brothers and sisters who by their courage, endurance and enterprise brought victory. May these qualities be yours as you grow up and join in the common effort to establish among the nations of the world unity and peace.

George R.I.

BIBLIOGRAPHY

Clark, Lloyd *Arnhem - Jumping the Rhine 1944-45*, 2008

Duffin, Kenneth *Fifty Years On, Romford Baptist Church*, 1984

Evans, Brian *Romford, Collier Row & Gidea Park*, 1994

Hill, Maureen *Britain At War*, 2003

Longmate, Norman *How We Lived Then*, 2002

Lucas Philips, C.E. *Cockleshell Heroes*, 1956

Man, John *Atlas of D-Day*, 1994

Mantanle, Ivor *History of World War II*, 1994

Patten, Marguerite *We'll Eat Again*, 1990

Rose-Price,Robin, Parnell,Jean *The Land They Left Behind*, 2004

Richards, Glyn *Ordeal in Romford, 1st edition,* 1945

Small, Ken *The Forgotten Dead*, 1988

Smith, F.D. *History of Electricity in Romford*, 1956, (unpublished)

Waller, Maureen *London 1945 - Life in the Debris of War*, 2004

Watt, Peter *Hitler v Havering*, 1994

Printed in Great Britain
by Amazon